Ethics

Other Books in the Current Controversies Series:

Chapter Preface

For centuries, philosophers, theologians, and other scholars have attempted to determine what factors motivate people to act ethically. Religion has frequently been cited as a primary force motivating ethical behavior. All religions contain specific ethical principles that believers are expected to follow. People may follow the ethical guidelines of their religion through fear of divine punishment if they transgress or in anticipation of being rewarded for leading a virtuous life.

Recently, however, some scientists have proposed that humans' sense of ethical behavior evolved through natural selection. They maintain that an individual's altruistic behavior, such as warning relatives of the approach of dangerous animals, increased the likelihood that these early humans would survive the threat and would live to pass on their altruistic genes to their descendants. According to this theory, humans are "hardwired" for ethical behavior.

The idea that humans may be biologically predisposed to ethical behavior is disturbing to many theologians and religious individuals. Even some scientists find the proposition unsettling, as Randolph Neese confesses: "The discovery that tendencies to altruism are shaped by benefits to genes is one of the most disturbing in the history of science. When I first grasped it, I slept badly for many nights, trying to find some alternative that did not so roughly challenge my sense of good and evil." According to author John Maynard Smith,

> Is there any way in which we can decide, with certainty, which actions are right? [There] is not, unless you hold that . . . human beings are here to do God's bidding. If a person is simply the product of his or her genetic makeup and environmental history, . . . there is simply no source whence absolute morality could come.

However, others assert that this scientific theory can be compatible with religious belief. For example, Christian author Larry Arnhart insists, "If God is the all-powerful and all-good Creator of nature, then there is no reason to believe that the natural constitution of human beings has been designed in opposition to moral goodness." According to this view, ethical behavior is motivated by a biological imperative that was given to humans by a divine creator.

Understanding the motivations behind ethical behavior is not simply a philosophical debate: These theories can influence society to adopt certain measures to encourage ethical behavior or to address chronic unethical behavior in individuals such as criminals. The contributors to the following chapter debate the answer to the lingering question of what causes humans to act ethically.

Belief in God Motivates People to Behave Ethically

by Benedict de Spinoza

About the author: *Benedict de Spinoza (1632–1677) was a Dutch philosopher. Born a Sephardic Jew, as a young man he was excommunicated from the Jewish community for his thoughts and practices. Spinoza proposed that people are guided by their own natures, and that virtuous people understand their own natures and ultimately seek to understand the nature of God. Spinoza wrote the books* A Treatise on Religious and Political Philosophy, Political Treatise, *and* Ethics, *from which this viewpoint is excerpted.*

I should like to say a few words about perfection and imperfection, and about good and evil. If a man has proposed to do a thing and has accomplished it, he calls it perfect, and not only he, but every one else who has really known or has believed that he has known the mind and intention of the author of that work will call it perfect too. For example, having seen some work (which I suppose to be as yet not finished), if we know that the intention of the author of that work is to build a house, we shall call the house imperfect; while, on the other hand, we shall call it perfect as soon as we see the work has been brought to the end which the author had determined for it. But if we see any work such as we have never seen before, and if we do not know the mind of the workman, we shall then not be able to say whether the work is perfect or imperfect. This seems to have been the first signification of these words; but afterwards men began to form universal ideas, to think out for themselves types of houses, buildings, castles, and to prefer some types of things to others; and so it happened that each person called a thing perfect which seemed to agree with the universal idea which he had formed of that thing, and, on the other hand, he called a thing imperfect which seemed to agree less with his typical conception, although, according to the intention of the workman, it had been entirely com-

Benedict de Spinoza, from *The Ethics of Spinoza*, translated by W.H. White and revised by A.H. Stirling. Reprinted by permission of Oxford University Press.

pleted. This appears to be the only reason why the words *perfect* and *imperfect* are commonly applied to natural objects which are not made with human hands; for men are in the habit of forming, both of natural as well as of artificial objects, universal ideas which they regard as types of things, and which they think nature has in view, setting them before herself as types too; it being the common opinion that she does noth-ing except for the sake of some end. When, therefore, men see something done by nature which does not alto-gether answer to that typal concep-

> *"The highest virtue of the mind is to understand or know God."*

tion which they have of the thing, they think that nature herself has failed or committed an error, and that she has left the thing imperfect. Thus we see that the custom of applying the words *perfect* and *imperfect* to natural objects has arisen rather from prejudice than from true knowledge of them. For . . . nature does nothing for the sake of an end, for that eternal and infinite Being whom we call God or Nature acts by the same necessity by which He exists; . . . He acts by the same necessity of nature as that by which He exists. The reason or cause, therefore, why God or nature acts and the reason why He exists are one and the same. Since, therefore, He exists for no end, He acts for no end; and since He has no principle or end of existence, He has no principle or end of ac-tion. A final cause, as it is called, is nothing, therefore, but human desire, in so far as this is considered as the principle or primary cause of anything. For ex-ample, when we say that the having a house to live in was the final cause of this or that house, we merely mean that a man, because he imagined the advantages of a domestic life, desired to build a house. Therefore, having a house to live in, in so far as it is considered as a final cause, is merely this particular desire, which is really an efficient cause, and is considered as primary, because men are usually ignorant of the causes of their desires; for, as I have often said, we are conscious of our actions and desires, but ignorant of the causes by which we are determined to desire anything. . . .

The Virtue of Knowing God

The highest good of the mind is the knowledge of God, and the highest virtue of the mind is to know God.

The highest thing which the mind can understand is God, that is to say, Being absolutely infinite, and without whom nothing can be nor can be conceived, and therefore that which is chiefly profitable to the mind, or which is the highest good of the mind, is the knowledge of God. Again, the mind acts only in so far as it understands, and only in so far can it be absolutely said to act in confor-mity with virtue. To understand, therefore, is the absolute virtue of the mind. But the highest thing which the mind can understand is God (as we have al-ready demonstrated), and therefore the highest virtue of the mind is to under-stand or know God. Q.E.D. . . .

The good which every one who follows after virtue seeks for himself he will desire for other men; and his desire on their behalf will be greater in proportion as he has a greater knowledge of God.

Men are most profitable to man in so far as they live according to the guidance of reason, and therefore, according to the guidance of reason, we necessarily endeavour to cause men to live according to the guidance of reason. But the good which each person seeks who lives according to the dictates of reason, that is to say, who follows after virtue, is to understand, and therefore the good which each person seeks who follows after virtue he will also desire for other men. Again, desire, in so far as it is related to the mind, is the essence itself of the mind. But the essence of the mind consists in knowledge, which involves the knowledge of God, and without this knowledge the essence of the mind can neither be nor be conceived; and therefore the greater the knowledge of God which the essence of the mind involves, the greater will be the desire with which he who follows after virtue will desire for another the good which he seeks for himself.   Q.E.D.

The good which a man seeks for himself and which he loves he will love more unchangeably if he sees that others love it, and therefore he will endeavour to make others love it; and because this good is common to all and all can rejoice in it, he will endeavour (by the same reasoning) to cause all to rejoice in it, and he will do so the more, the more he rejoices in this good himself. Q.E.D.

He who strives from an affect alone to make others love what he himself loves, and to make others live according to his way of thinking, acts from mere impulse, and is therefore hateful, especially to those who have other tastes and who therefore also desire, and by the same impulse strive to make others live according to their way of thinking.

Again, since the highest good which men seek from an affect is often such that only one person can possess it, it follows that persons who love are not consistent with themselves, and, whilst they delight to recount the praises of the beloved object, fear lest they should be believed. But he who endeavours to lead others by reason does not act from impulse, but with humanity and kindness, and is always consistent with himself.

The Guidance of Reason

Everything which we desire and do, of which we are the cause in so far as we possess an idea of God, or in so far as we know God, I refer to *Religion*. The desire of doing well which is born in us, because we live according to the guidance of reason, I call *Piety*. The desire to join others in friendship to himself, with which a man living according to the guidance of reason is possessed, I call

> *"The good which each person seeks who follows after virtue he will also desire for other men."*

Chapter 1

Honour. I call that thing *Honourable* which men who live according to the guidance of reason praise; and that thing, on the contrary, I call *Base* which sets itself against the formation of friendship. . . .

It is by the highest right of nature that each person exists, and consequently it is by the highest right of nature that each person does those things which follow from the necessity of his nature; and therefore it is by the highest right of nature that each person judges what is good and what is evil, consults his own advantage as he thinks best, avenges himself, and endeavours to preserve what he loves and to destroy what he hates. If men lived according to the guidance of reason, every one would enjoy this right without injuring any one else. But because men are subject to affects, which far surpass human power or virtue, they are often drawn in different directions, and are contrary to one another, although they need one another's help.

In order, then, that men may be able to live in harmony and be a help to one another, it is necessary for them to cede their natural right, and beget confidence one in the other that they will do nothing by which one can injure the other.

Atheism Motivates People to Behave Ethically

by Friedrich Nietzsche

About the author: *Friedrich Nietzsche (1844–1900) was a German philosopher, author, and poet. He is renowned for his statement, "God is dead," by which he meant that religion had lost its meaningfulness and efficacy in modern society. He rejected Christianity, arguing that its values were based on fear and resentment, that it incorrectly accepted all people as equals, and that it denied this world in favor of an illusory other world. Nietzsche's concept of the "superman"—the passionate individual able to control and utilize passions creatively—expressed his view of the ideal manner of human existence. He wrote the books* Thus Spake Zarathustra *and* Beyond Good and Evil, *from which this viewpoint is excerpted.*

The human soul and its frontiers, the compass of human inner experience in general attained hitherto, the heights, depths and distances of this experience, the entire history of the soul *hitherto* and its still unexhausted possibilities: this is the predestined hunting-ground for a born psychologist and lover of the "big-game hunt." But how often must he say despairingly to himself: "one man! alas, but one man! and this great forest and jungle!" And thus he wishes he had a few hundred beaters and subtle well-instructed tracker dogs whom he could send into the history of the human soul and there round up *his* game. In vain: he discovers again and again, thoroughly and bitterly, how hard it is to find beaters and dogs for all the things which arouse his curiosity. The drawback in sending scholars out into new and dangerous hunting grounds where courage, prudence, subtlety in every sense are needed is that they cease to be of any use precisely where the "*big* hunt," but also the big danger, begins—precisely there they do lose their keenness of eye and keenness of nose. To divine and establish, for example, what sort of history the problem of *knowledge and conscience* has had in the soul of *homines religiosi* one would oneself perhaps have to be as profound, as wounded, as monstrous as Pascal's intellectual conscience was—and

Excerpted from Friedrich Nietzsche, *Beyond Good and Evil*, translated by R.J. Hollingdale. London: Penguin Classics, 1973. Translation ©1972 by R.J. Hollingdale. Reprinted by permission of Penguin Books Ltd.

then there would still be needed that broad heaven of bright, malicious spirituality capable of looking down on this turmoil of dangerous and painful experiences, surveying and ordering them and forcing them into formulas.—But who could do me this service! And who could have the time to wait for such servants!—They appear too rarely, they are at all times so very improbable! In the end one has to do everything *oneself* if one is to know a few things oneself: that is to say, one has *much* to do!—But a curiosity like mine is after all the most pleasurable of vices—I beg your pardon! I meant to say: the love of truth has its reward in Heaven, and already upon earth.—

Suicide of Reason

The faith such as primitive Christianity demanded and not infrequently obtained in the midst of a sceptical and southerly free-spirited world with a centuries-long struggle between philosophical schools behind it and in it, plus the education in tolerance provided by the *Imperium Romanum*—this faith is *not* that gruff, true-hearted liegeman's faith with which a Martin Luther, say, or an Oliver Cromwell, or some other northern barbarian of the spirit cleaved to his God and his Christianity; it is rather that faith of Pascal which resembles in a terrible fashion a protracted suicide of reason—of a tough, long-lived, worm-like reason which is not to be killed instantaneously with a single blow. The Christian faith is from the beginning sacrifice: sacrifice of all freedom, all pride, all self-confidence of the spirit, at the same time enslavement and self-mockery, self-mutilation. There is cruelty and religious Phoenicianism in this faith exacted of an over-ripe, manifold and much-indulged conscience: its presupposition is that the subjection of the spirit is indescribably *painful*, that the entire past and habitude of such a spirit resists the *absurdissimum* which "faith" appears to it to be. Modern men, with their obtuseness to all Christian nomenclature, no longer sense the gruesome superlative which lay for an antique taste in the paradoxical formula "god on the cross." Never and nowhere has there hitherto been a comparable boldness in inversion, anything so fearsome, questioning and questionable, as this formula: it promised a reevaluation of all antique values.—It is the orient, the *innermost* orient, it is the oriental slave who in this fashion took vengeance on Rome and its noble and frivolous tolerance on Roman "catholicism" of faith; and it has never been faith but always freedom from faith, that half-stoical and smiling unconcern with the seriousness of faith, that has enraged slaves in their masters and against their masters. "Enlightenment" enrages: for the slave who wants the unconditional, he understands in the domain of morality too only the tyrannical, he loves as he hates, without nuance, into the depths of him, to the point of pain, to the point of sickness—the great hid-

> *"The Christian faith is . . . sacrifice of all freedom, all pride, all self-confidence of the spirit."*

21

den suffering he feels is enraged at the noble taste which seems to *deny* suffering. Scepticism towards suffering, at bottom no more than a pose of aristocratic morality, was likewise not the least contributory cause of the last great slave revolt which began with the French Revolution.

The Dangers of Christianity

Wherever the religious neurosis has hitherto appeared on earth we find it tied to three dangerous dietary prescriptions: solitude, fasting and sexual abstinence—but without our being able to decide with certainty which is cause here and which effect, or *whether* any relation of cause and effect is involved here at all. The justification of the latter doubt is that one of the most frequent symptoms of the condition, in the case of savage and tame peoples, is the most sudden and most extravagant voluptuousness which is then, just as suddenly, reversed into a convulsion of penitence and a denial of world and will: both perhaps interpretable as masked epilepsy? But nowhere is it more necessary to renounce interpretations: around no other type has there grown up such an abundance of nonsense and superstition, none seems to have hitherto interested men, even philosophers, more—the time has come to cool down a little on this matter, to learn caution: better to look away, *to go away.* . . .

It seems that their Catholicism is much more an intrinsic part of the Latin races than the whole of Christianity in general is of us northerners; and that unbelief consequently signifies something altogether different in Catholic countries from what it does in Protestant—namely a kind of revolt against the spirit of the race,

> *"Why atheism today?—'The father' in God is thoroughly refuted.* . . . *He does not hear—and if he heard he would still not know how to help."*

while with us it is rather a return to the spirit (or lack of spirit—) of the race. We northerners are undoubtedly descended from barbarian races also in respect of our talent for religion: we have *little* talent for it. We may except the Celts, who therefore supplied the best soil for the reception of the Christian infection in the north—the Christian ideal came to blossom, so far as the pale northern sun permitted it, in France. How uncongenially pious are to our taste even these latest French sceptics when they have in them any Celtic blood! How Catholic, how un-German does August Comte's sociology smell to us with its Roman logic of the instincts! How Jesuitical that clever and charming cicerone of Port-Royal, Charles-Augustin Sainte-Beuve, despite all his hostility towards the Jesuits! And even more so Ernest Renan: how inaccessible to us notherners is the language of a Renan, in whom every other minute some nothingness of religious tension topples a soul which is in a refined sense voluptuous and relaxed! . . .

What astonishes one about the religiosity of the ancient Greeks is the tremendous amount of gratitude that emanates from it—the kind of man who stands *thus* before nature and before life is a very noble one!—Later, when the rabble came to predominate in Greece, *fear* also overran religion; and Christianity was preparing itself.—

The passion for God: there is the peasant, true-hearted and importunate kind, like Luther's—the whole of Protestantism lacks southern *delicatezza*. There is an oriental ecstatic kind, like that of a slave who has been undeservedly pardoned and elevated, as for example in the case of Augustine, who lacks in an offensive manner all nobility of bearing and desire. There

> *"The concepts 'God' and 'sin' will one day seem to us of no more importance than a child's toy and a child's troubles seem to an old man."*

is the womanly tender and longing kind which presses bashfully and ignorantly for a *unio mystica et physica*: as in the case of Madame de Guyon. In many cases it appears strangely enough as a disguise for the puberty of a girl or a youth; now and then even as the hysteria of an old maid, also as her final ambition—the church has more than once canonized the woman in question.

Hitherto the mightiest men have still bowed down reverently before the saint as the enigma of self-constraint and voluntary final renunciation: why did they bow? They sensed in him—as it were behind the question-mark presented by his fragile and miserable appearance—the superior force that sought to prove itself through such a constraint, the strength of will in which they recognized and knew how to honour their own strength and joy in ruling: they honoured something in themselves when they honoured the saint. In addition to this, the sight of the saint aroused a suspicion in them: such an enormity of denial, of anti-nature, will not have been desired for nothing, they said to themselves. Is there perhaps a reason for it, a very great danger about which the ascetic, thanks to his secret visitors and informants, might possess closer knowledge? Enough, the mighty world learned in face of him a new fear, they sensed a new power, a strange enemy as yet unsubdued—it was the "will to power" which constrained them to halt before the saint. They had to question him—.

In the Jewish "Old Testament," the book of divine justice, there are men, things and speeches of so grand a style that Greek and Indian literature have nothing to set beside it. One stands in reverence and trembling before these remnants of what man once was and has sorrowful thoughts about old Asia and its little jutting-out promontory Europe, which would like to signify as against Asia the "progress of man." To be sure: he who is only a measly tame domestic animal and knows only the needs of a domestic animal (like our cultured people of today, the Christians of "cultured" Christianity included—) has no reason to wonder, let alone to sorrow, among those ruins—the taste for the Old Testament is a touchstone in regard to "great" and "small"—: perhaps he will find the New Testament, the book of mercy, more after his own heart (there is in it a great deal of the genuine delicate, musty odour of devotee and petty soul). To have glued this New Testament, a species of rococo taste in every respect, on to the Old Testament to form a *single* book, as "bible," as "the book of books": that is perhaps the greatest piece of temerity and "sin against the spirit" that literary Europe has on its conscience.

Why Atheism?

Why atheism today?—"The father" in God is thoroughly refuted; likewise "the judge," "the rewarder." Likewise his "free will": he does not hear—and if he heard he would still not know how to help. The worst thing is: he seems incapable of making himself clearly understood: is he himself vague about what he means?—These are what, in course of many conversations, asking and listening, I found to be the causes of the decline of European theism; it seems to me that the religious instinct is indeed in vigorous growth—but that it rejects the theistic answer with profound mistrust. . . .

There is a great ladder of religious cruelty with many rungs; but three of them are the most important. At one time one sacrificed human beings to one's god, perhaps precisely those human beings one loved best—the sacrifice of the first-born present in all prehistoric religions belongs here, as does the sacrifice of the Emperor Tiberius in the Mithras grotto on the isle of Capri, that most horrible of all Roman anachronisms. Then, in the moral epoch of mankind, one sacrificed to one's god the strongest instincts one possessed, one's "nature"; the joy of *this* festival glitters in the cruel glance of the ascetic, the inspired "anti-naturist." Finally: what was left to be sacrificed? Did one not finally have to sacrifice everything comforting, holy, healing, all hope, all faith in a concealed harmony, in a future bliss and justice? Did one not have to sacrifice God himself and out of cruelty against oneself worship stone, stupidity, gravity, fate, nothingness? To sacrifice God for nothingness—this paradoxical mystery of the ultimate act of cruelty was reserved for the generation which is even now arising: we all know something of it already.—

He who, prompted by some enigmatic desire, has, like me, long endeavoured to think pessimism through to the bottom and to redeem it from the half-Christian, half-German simplicity and narrowness with which it finally presented itself to this century, namely in the form of the Schopenhaueran philosophy; he who has really gazed with an Asiatic and more than Asiatic eye down into the most world-denying of all possible modes of thought—beyond good and evil and no longer, like Buddha and Arthur Schopenhauer, under the spell and illusion of morality—perhaps by that very act, and without really intending to, may have had his eyes opened to the opposite ideal: to the ideal of the most exuberant, most living and most world-affirming man, who has not only learned to get on and treat with all that was and is but who wants to have it again *as it was and is* to all

> **"What wisdom there is in the fact that men are superficial."**

eternity, insatiably calling out *da capo* not only to himself, but to the whole piece and play, and not only to a play but fundamentally to him who needs precisely this play—and who makes it necessary: because he needs himself again and again—and makes himself necessary—What? And would this not be—*circulus vitiosus deus?*

> **"Piety . . . [is] the subtlest and ultimate product of the fear of truth."**

With the strength of his spiritual sight and insight the distance, and as it were the space, around man continually expands: his world grows deeper, ever new stars, ever new images and enigmas come into view. Perhaps everything on which the spirit's eye has exercised its profundity and acuteness has been really but an opportunity for its exercise, a game, something for children and the childish. Perhaps the most solemn concepts which have occasioned the most strife and suffering, the concepts "God" and "sin," will one day seem to us of no more importance than a child's toy and a child's troubles seem to an old man—and perhaps "old man" will then have need of another toy and other troubles—still enough of a child, an eternal child!

Indifference to Religion

Has it been observed to what extent a genuine religious life (both for its favourite labour of microscopic self-examination and that gentle composure which calls itself "prayer" and which is a constant readiness for the "coming of God"—) requires external leisure or semi-leisure, I mean leisure with a good conscience, inherited, by blood, which is not altogether unfamiliar with the aristocratic idea that work *degrades*—that is to say, makes soul and body common? And that consequently modern, noisy, time-consuming, proud and stupidly proud industriousness educates and prepares precisely for "unbelief" more than anything else does? Among those in Germany for example who nowadays live without religion, I find people whose "free-thinking" is of differing kinds and origins but above all a majority for those in whom industriousness from generation to generation has extinguished the religious instincts: so that they no longer have any idea what religions are supposed to be for and as it were merely register their existence in the world with a kind of dumb amazement. They feel they are already fully occupied, these worthy people, whether with their businesses or with their pleasures, not to speak of the "fatherland" and the newspapers and "family duties": it seems that they have no time at all left for religion, especially as it is not clear to them whether it involves another business or another pleasure—for they tell themselves it is not possible that one goes to church simply to make oneself miserable. They are not opposed to religious usages; if participation in such usages is demanded in certain cases, by the state for instance, they do what is demanded of them as one does so many things—with patient and modest seriousness and without much curiosity and discomfort—it is only that they live too much aside and outside even to feel the need for any for or against in such things. The great majority of German middle-class Protestants can today be numbered among these indifferent people, especially in the great industrious centres of trade and commerce; likewise the great majority of industrious scholars and the entire university equipage (excepting the theologians, whose possibility and presence there provides the psychologist with ever more and ever subtler enigmas to solve). Pious or even merely church-going people seldom realize *how much* good will, one might even say willfulness, it requires nowadays for a German scholar to take the problem of religion seriously; his whole trade (and as said above, the tradesmanlike industriousness to which his modern conscience obliges him) disposes him to a superior, almost good-natured merriment in regard to religion, sometimes mixed with a mild contempt directed at the "uncleanliness" of spirit which he presupposes wherever one still belongs to the church. It is only with the aid of history (thus *not* from his personal experience) that the scholar succeeds in summoning up a reverent seriousness and a certain shy respect towards religion; but if he intensifies his feelings towards it even to the point of feeling grateful to it, he has still in his own person not got so much as a single step closer to that which still exists as church or piety: perhaps the reverse. The practical indifference to religious things in which he was born and raised is as a rule sublimated in him into a caution and cleanliness which avoids contact with religious people

> *"Christianity has been the most fatal kind of self-presumption ever."*

and things; and it can be precisely the depth of his tolerance and humanity that bids him evade the subtle distress which tolerance itself brings with it.—Every age has its own divine kind of naïvety for the invention of which other ages may envy it—and how much naïvety, venerable, childlike and boundlessly stupid naïvety there is in the scholar's belief in his superiority, in the good conscience of his tolerance, in the simple unsuspecting certainty with which his instinct treats the religious man as an inferior and lower type which he himself has grown beyond and *above*—he, the little presumptuous dwarf and man of the mob, the brisk and busy head- and handyman of "ideas," of "modern ideas"!

Fear Leads People to Religion

He who has seen deeply into the world knows what wisdom there is in the fact that men are superficial. It is their instinct for preservation which teaches them to be fickle, light and false. Here and there, among philosophers as well as artists, one finds a passionate and exaggerated worship of "pure forms": let no one doubt that he who *needs* the cult of surfaces to that extent has at some time or other made a calamitous attempt to get *beneath* them. Perhaps there might even exist an order of rank in regard to these burnt children, these born artists who can find pleasure in life only in the intention of falsifying its image (as it were in a long-drawn-out revenge on life—): one could determine the degree to which life has been spoiled for them by the extent to which they want to see its image falsified, attenuated and made otherworldly and divine—one could include the *homines religiosi* among the artists as their *highest* rank. It is the profound suspicious fear of an incurable pessimism which compels whole millennia to cling with their teeth to a religious interpretation of existence: the fear born of that instinct which senses that one might get hold of the truth *too soon*, before mankind was sufficiently strong, sufficiently hard,

> *"A shrunken, almost ludicrous species, a herd animal, something full of good will, sickly and mediocre has been bred, the European of today."*

sufficient of an artist. . . . Piety, the "life in God," would, viewed in this light, appear as the subtlest and ultimate product of the *fear* of truth, as the artist's worship of an intoxication before the most consistent of all falsifications, as the will to inversion of truth, to untruth at any price. Perhaps there has up till now been no finer way of making man himself more beautiful than piety: through piety man can become to so great a degree art, surface, play of colours, goodness, that one no longer suffers at the sight of him.—

To love men *for the sake of God*—that has been the noblest and most remote feeling attained to among men up till now. That love of man without some sanctifying ulterior objective is one piece of stupidity and animality *more*, that the inclination to this love of man has first to receive its measure, its refinement, its grain of salt and drop of amber from a higher inclination—whatever man it was who first felt and "experienced" this, however much his tongue may have faltered as it sought to express such a delicate thought, let him be holy and venerated to us for all time as the man who has soared the highest and gone the most beautifully astray! . . .

The Danger of Saving the Weak

Among men, as among every other species, there is a surplus of failures, of the sick, the degenerate, the fragile, of those who are bound to suffer. . . . Now what is the attitude of [Christianity and Buddhism] towards this *surplus* of unsuccessful cases? They seek to preserve, to retain in life, whatever can in any way be preserved, indeed they side with it as a matter of principle as religions *for sufferers*, they maintain that all those who suffer from life as from an illness are in the right, and would like every other feeling of life to be counted false and become impossible. However highly one may rate this kindly preservative solicitude, inasmuch as, together with all the other types of man, it has been and is applied to the highest type, which has hitherto almost always been the type that has suffered most: in the total accounting the hitherto *sovereign* religions are among the main reasons the type "man" has been kept on a lower level—they have preserved too much of that *which ought to perish*. We have inestimable benefits to thank them for; and who is sufficiently rich in gratitude not to be impoverished in face of all that the "spiritual men" of Christianity, for example, have hitherto done for Europe! And yet, when they gave comfort to the suffering, courage to the oppressed and despairing, a staff and stay to the irresolute, and lured those who were inwardly shattered and had become savage away from society into monasteries and houses of correction for the soul: what did they have to do in addition so as thus, with a good conscience, as a matter of principle, to work at the preservation of everything sick and suffering, which means in fact and truth at the *corruption of the European race?* Stand all evaluations *on their head—that* is what they had to do! And smash the strong, contaminate great hopes, cast suspicion on joy in beauty, break down everything autocratic, manly, conquering, tyrannical, all the instincts proper to the highest and most successful of the type "man," into uncertainty, remorse of conscience, self-destruction, indeed reverse the whole love of the earthly and of dominion over the earth into hatred of the earth and the earthly—*that* is the task the church set itself and had to set itself, until in its evaluation "unworldliness," "unsensuality," and "higherman" were finally fused together into *one* feeling. Supposing one were able to view the strangely painful and at the same time coarse and subtle comedy of European Christianity with the mocking and unconcerned eye of an Epicurean god, I believe there would be no end to one's laughter and amazement: for does it not seem that *one* will has dominated Europe for eighteen centuries, the will to make of man a *sublime abortion?* But he who, with an opposite desire, no longer Epicurean but with some divine hammer in his hand, approached this almost deliberate degeneration and stunting of man such as constitutes the European Christian (Pascal for instance), would he not have to cry out in rage, in pity, in horror: "O you fools, you presumptuous, pitying fools, what have you done! Was this a work for your hands! How you have bungled and botched my beautiful stone! What a thing for *you* to take upon yourselves!"—What I am saying is: Christianity has been the most fatal kind of self-presumption ever. Men not high or hard enough for the artistic refashioning of *mankind*; men not strong or farsighted enough for the sublime self-constraint needed to *allow* the foreground law of thousandfold failure and perishing to prevail; men not noble enough to see the abysmal disparity in order of rank and abysm of rank between man and man—it is *such* men who, with their "equal before God," have hitherto ruled over the destiny of Europe, until at last a shrunken, almost ludicrous species, a herd animal, something full of good will, sickly and mediocre has been bred, the European of today.

Biological Imperative Causes People to Act Ethically

by Edward O. Wilson

About the author: *Scientist and author Edward O. Wilson is the Pellegrino University Research Professor at Harvard University, as well as Honorary Curator in Entomology for Harvard's Museum of Comparative Zoology. His books include* The Diversity of Life, On Human Nature, *and* Consilience: The Unity of Knowledge, *from which the following viewpoint is adapted.*

Centuries of debate on the origin of ethics come down to this: Either ethical principles, such as justice and human rights, are independent of human experience, or they are human inventions. The distinction is more than an exercise for academic philosophers. The choice between these two understandings makes all the difference in the way we view ourselves as a species. It measures the authority of religion, and it determines the conduct of moral reasoning.

Competing Assumptions

The two assumptions in competition are like islands in a sea of chaos, as different as life and death, matter and the void. One cannot learn which is correct by pure logic; the answer will eventually be reached through an accumulation of objective evidence. Moral reasoning, I believe, is at every level intrinsically consilient with—compatible with, intertwined with—the natural sciences. (I use a form of the word "consilience"—literally a "jumping together" of knowledge as a result of the linking of facts and fact-based theory across disciplines to create a common groundwork of explanation—because its rarity has preserved its precision.)

Every thoughtful person has an opinion on which premise is correct. But the split is not, as popularly supposed, between religious believers and secularists. It is between transcendentalists, who think that moral guidelines exist outside the human mind, and empiricists, who think them contrivances of the mind. In simplest terms, the options are as follows: *I believe in the independence of moral values, whether from God or not,* and *I believe that moral values come from human beings alone, whether or not God exists.*

Theologians and philosophers have almost always focused on transcendentalism as the means to validate ethics. They seek the grail of natural law, which comprises freestanding principles of moral conduct immune to doubt and compromise. Christian theologians, following Saint Thomas Aquinas's reasoning in *Summa Theologiae,* by and large consider natural

> *"If we explore the biological roots of moral behavior, . . . we should be able to fashion a wise and enduring ethical consensus."*

law to be an expression of God's will. In this view, human beings have an obligation to discover the law by diligent reasoning and to weave it into the routine of their daily lives. Secular philosophers of a transcendental bent may seem to be radically different from theologians, but they are actually quite similar, at least in moral reasoning. They tend to view natural law as a set of principles so powerful, whatever their origin, as to be self-evident to any rational person. In short, transcendental views are fundamentally the same whether God is invoked or not. . . .

The Empiricist View of Ethics

In the empiricist view, ethics is conduct favored consistently enough throughout a society to be expressed as a code of principles. It reaches its precise form in each culture according to historical circumstance. The codes, whether adjudged good or evil by outsiders, play an important role in determining which cultures flourish and which decline.

The crux of the empiricist view is its emphasis on objective knowledge. Because the success of an ethical code depends on how wisely it interprets moral sentiments, those who frame one should know how the brain works, and how the mind develops. The success of ethics also depends on how accurately a society can predict the consequences of particular actions as opposed to others, especially in cases of moral ambiguity.

The empiricist argument holds that if we explore the biological roots of moral behavior, and explain their material origins and biases, we should be able to fashion a wise and enduring ethical consensus. The current expansion of scientific inquiry into the deeper processes of human thought makes this venture feasible. . . .

I am an empiricist. On religion I lean toward deism, but consider its proof largely a problem in astrophysics. The existence of a God who created the universe (as envisioned by deism) is possible, and the question may eventually be settled, perhaps by forms of material evidence not yet imagined. Or the matter may be forever beyond human reach. In contrast, and of far greater importance to humanity, the idea of a biological God, one who directs organic evolution and intervenes in human affairs (as envisioned by theism), is increasingly contravened by biology and the brain sciences.

The same evidence, I believe, favors a purely material origin of ethics, and it meets the criterion of consilience: causal explanations of brain activity and evolution, while imperfect, already cover most facts known about behavior we term "moral.". . .

The argument of the empiricist has roots that go back to Aristotle's *Nicomachean Ethics* and, in the beginning of the modern era, to David Hume's *A Treatise of Human Nature* (1739–1740). The first clear evolutionary elaboration of it was by Charles Darwin, in *The Descent of Man* (1871). . . .

[In the empiricist view,] the individual is seen as predisposed biologically to make certain choices. Through cultural evolution some of the choices are hardened into precepts, then into laws, and, if the predisposition or coercion is strong enough, into a belief in the command of God or the natural order of the universe. The general empiricist principle takes this form: *Strong innate feeling and historical experience cause certain actions to be preferred; we have experienced them, and have weighed their consequences, and agree to conform with codes that express them. Let us take an oath upon the codes, invest our personal honor in them, and suffer punishment for their violation.* The empiricist view concedes that moral codes are devised to conform to some drives of human nature and to suppress others. *Ought* is the translation not of human nature but of the public will, which

> **"Causal explanations of brain activity and evolution . . . cover most facts known about behavior we term 'moral.'"**

can be made increasingly wise and stable through an understanding of the needs and pitfalls of human nature. The empiricist view recognizes that the strength of commitment can wane as a result of new knowledge and experience, with the result that certain rules may be desacralized, old laws rescinded, and formerly prohibited behavior set free. It also recognizes that for the same reason new moral codes may need to be devised, with the potential of being made sacred in time.

The Origin of Moral Instincts

If the empiricist world view is correct, *ought* is just shorthand for one kind of factual statement, a word that denotes what society first chose (or was coerced) to do, and then codified. The naturalistic fallacy is thereby reduced to the naturalistic problem. The solution of the problem is not difficult: *ought* is the product of a material process. The solution points the way to an objective grasp of the origin of ethics.

A few investigators are now embarked on just such a foundational inquiry. Most agree that ethical codes have arisen by evolution through the interplay of biology and culture. . . .

What have been thought of as moral sentiments are now taken to mean moral instincts (as defined by the modern behavioral sciences), subject to judgment according to their consequences. Such sentiments are thus derived from epigenetic rules—hereditary biases in mental development, usually conditioned by emotion, that influence concepts and decisions made from them. The primary origin of moral instincts is the dynamic relation between cooperation and defection. The essential ingredient for the molding of the instincts during genetic evolution in any species is intelligence high enough to judge and manipulate the tension generated by the dynamism. That level of intelligence allows the building of complex mental scenarios well into the future. It occurs, so far as is known, only in human beings and perhaps their closest relatives among the higher apes.

A way of envisioning the hypothetical earliest stages of moral evolution is provided by game theory, particularly the solutions to the famous Prisoner's Dilemma. Consider the following typical scenario of the dilemma. Two gang members have been arrested for murder and are being questioned separately. The evidence against them is strong but not irrefutable. The first gang member believes that if he turns state's witness, he will be granted immunity and his partner will be sentenced to life in prison. But he is also aware that his partner has the same option, and that if both of them exercise it, neither will be granted immunity. That is the dilemma. Will the two gang members independently defect, so that both take the hard fall? They will not, because they agreed in advance to remain silent if caught. By doing so, both hope to be convicted on a lesser charge or escape punishment altogether. Criminal gangs have turned this principle of calculation into an ethical precept: Never rat on another member; always be a stand-up guy. Honor does exist among thieves. The gang is a society of sorts; its code is the same as that of a captive soldier in wartime, obliged to give only name, rank, and serial number.

The Benefits of Cooperation

In one form or another, comparable dilemmas that are solvable by cooperation occur constantly and everywhere in daily life. The payoff is variously money, status, power, sex, access, comfort, or health. Most of these proximate rewards are converted into the universal bottom line of Darwinian genetic fitness: greater longevity and a secure, growing family.

And so it has most likely always been. Imagine a Paleolithic band of five hunters. One considers breaking away from the others to look for an antelope on his own. If successful, he will gain a large quantity of meat and hide—five times as much as if he stays with the band and they are successful. But he knows from experience that his

> *"Moral codes are devised to conform to some drives of human nature and to suppress others."*

chances of success are very low, much less than the chances of the band of five working together. In addition, whether successful alone or not, he will suffer animosity from the others for lessening their prospects. By custom the band members remain together and share equitably the animals they kill. So the hunter stays. He also observes good manners in doing so, especially if he is the one who makes the kill. Boastful pride is condemned, because it rips the delicate web of reciprocity.

> *"Ethical codes have arisen by evolution through the interplay of biology and culture."*

Now suppose that human propensities to cooperate or defect are heritable: some people are innately more cooperative, others less so. In this respect moral aptitude would simply be like almost all other mental traits studied to date. Among traits with documented heritability, those closest to moral aptitude are empathy with the distress of others and certain processes of attachment between infants and their caregivers. To the heritability of moral aptitude add the abundant evidence of history that cooperative individuals generally survive longer and leave more offspring. Following that reasoning, in the course of evolutionary history genes predisposing people toward cooperative behavior would have come to predominate in the human population as a whole.

Such a process repeated through thousands of generations inevitably gave rise to moral sentiments. With the exception of psychopaths (if any truly exist), every person vividly experiences these instincts variously as conscience, self-respect, remorse, empathy, shame, humility, and moral outrage. They bias cultural evolution toward the conventions that express the universal moral codes of honor, patriotism, altruism, justice, compassion, mercy, and redemption.

The dark side of the inborn propensity to moral behavior is xenophobia. Because personal familiarity and common interest are vital in social transactions, moral sentiments evolved to be selective. People give trust to strangers with effort, and true compassion is a commodity in chronically short supply. Tribes cooperate only through carefully defined treaties and other conventions. They are quick to imagine themselves the victims of conspiracies by competing groups, and they are prone to dehumanize and murder their rivals during periods of severe conflict. They cement their own group loyalties by means of sacred symbols and ceremonies. Their mythologies are filled with epic victories over menacing enemies.

The complementary instincts of morality and tribalism are easily manipulated. Civilization has made them more so. Beginning about 10,000 years ago, a tick in geological time, when the agricultural revolution started in the Middle East, in China, and in Mesoamerica, populations increased tenfold in density over those of hunter-gatherer societies. Families settled on small plots of land, villages proliferated, and labor was finely divided as a growing minority of the populace specialized as craftsmen, traders, and soldiers. The rising agricultural societies became increasingly hierarchical. As chiefdoms and then states thrived on agricultural surpluses, hereditary rulers and priestly castes took power. The old ethical codes were transformed into coercive regulations, always to the advantage of the ruling classes. About this time the idea of law-giving gods originated. Their commands lent the ethical codes overpowering authority—once again, no surprise, in the interests of the rulers.

The Complexity of Human Nature

Because of the technical difficulty of analyzing such phenomena in an objective manner, and because people resist biological explanations of their higher cortical functions in the first place, very little progress has been made in the biological exploration of the moral sentiments. Even so, it is astonishing that the study of ethics has advanced so little since the nineteenth century. The most distinguishing and vital qualities of the human species remain a blank space on the scientific map. I doubt that discussions of ethics should rest upon the freestanding assumptions of contemporary philosophers who have evidently never given thought to the evolutionary origin and material functioning of the human brain. In no other domain of the humanities is a union with the natural sciences more urgently needed.

"What have been thought of as moral sentiments are now taken to mean moral instincts."

When the ethical dimension of human nature is at last fully opened to such exploration, the innate epigenetic rules of moral reasoning will probably not prove to be aggregated into simple instincts such as bonding, cooperativeness, and altruism. Instead the rules will most probably turn out to be an ensemble of many algorithms, whose interlocking activities guide the mind across a landscape of nuanced moods and choices.

Such a prestructured mental world may at first seem too complicated to have been created by autonomous genetic evolution alone. But all the evidence of biology suggests that just this process was enough to spawn the millions of species of life surrounding us. Each kind of animal is furthermore guided through its life cycle by unique and often elaborate sets of instinctual algorithms, many of which are beginning to yield to genetic and neurobiological analyses. With all these examples before us, we may reasonably conclude that human behavior originated the same way. . . .

The Origins of Religion

The same reasoning that aligns ethical philosophy with science can also inform the study of religion. Religions are analogous to organisms. They have a life cycle. They are born, they grow, they compete, they reproduce, and, in the fullness of time, most die. In each of these phases religions reflect the human organisms that nourish them. They express a primary rule of human existence:

Whatever is necessary to sustain life is also ultimately biological.

Successful religions typically begin as cults, which then increase in power and inclusiveness until they achieve tolerance outside the circle of believers. At the core of each religion is a creation myth, which explains how the world began and how the chosen people—those subscribing to the belief system—arrived at its center. Often a mystery, a set of secret instructions and formulas, is available to members who have worked their way to a higher state of enlightenment. The medieval Jewish cabala, the trigradal system of Freemasonry, and the carvings on Australian aboriginal spirit sticks are examples of such arcana. Power radiates from the center, gathering converts and binding followers to the group. Sacred places are designated, where the gods can be importuned, rites observed, and miracles witnessed.

The devotees of the religion compete as a tribe with those of other religions. They harshly resist the dismissal of their beliefs by rivals. They venerate self-sacrifice in defense of the religion.

The tribalistic roots of religion are similar to those of moral reasoning and may be identical. Religious rites, such as burial ceremonies, are very old. It appears that in the late Paleolithic period in Europe and the Middle East bodies were sometimes placed in shallow graves, accompanied by ocher or blossoms; one can easily imagine such ceremonies performed to invoke spirits and gods. But, as theoretical deduction and the evidence suggest, the primitive elements of moral behavior are far older than Paleolithic ritual. Religion arose on a foundation of ethics, and it has probably always been used in one manner or another to justify moral codes.

Religion and Instincts

The formidable influence of the religious drive is based on far more, however, than just the validation of morals. A great subterranean river of the mind, it gathers strength from a broad spread of tributary emotions. Foremost among them is the survival instinct. "Fear," as the Roman poet Lucretius said, "was the first thing on earth to make the gods." Our conscious minds hunger for a permanent existence. If we cannot have everlasting life of the body, then absorption into some immortal whole will serve. *Anything* will serve, as long as it gives the individual meaning and somehow stretches into eternity that swift passage of the mind and spirit lamented by Saint Augustine as the short day of time.

"Cooperative individuals generally survive longer and leave more offspring."

The understanding and control of life is another source of religious power. Doctrine draws on the same creative springs as science and the arts, its aim being the extraction of order from the mysteries and tumult of the material world. To explain the meaning of life it spins mythic narratives of the tribal history, populating the cosmos with protective spirits and gods. The existence of the supernatural, if accepted, testifies to the existence of that other world so desperately desired.

Religion is also mightily empowered by its principal ally, tribalism. The shamans and priests implore us, in somber cadence, *Trust in the sacred rituals, become part of the immortal force, you are one of us. As your life unfolds, each step has mystic signifi- cance that we who love you will mark*

> **"The dark side of the inborn propensity to moral behavior is xenophobia."**

with a solemn rite of passage, the last to be performed when you enter that sec- ond world, free of pain and fear.

If the religious mythos did not exist in a culture, it would quickly be invented, and in fact it has been invented everywhere, thousands of times through history. Such inevitability is the mark of instinctual behavior in any species, which is guided toward certain states by emotion-driven rules of mental development. To call religion instinctive is not to suppose that any particular part of its mythos is untrue—only that its sources run deeper than ordinary habit and are in fact hereditary, urged into existence through biases in mental development that are encoded in the genes.

Biological Imperative Does Not Cause People to Act Ethically

by Philip Yancey

About the author: *Philip Yancey is a columnist for* Christianity Today *and a frequent contributor to* Books & Culture *and other magazines. He is also the author of numerous books, including* What's So Amazing About Grace? *and* The Jesus I Never Knew.

A representative of Generation X named Sam told me he had been discovering the strategic advantages of truth. As an experiment, he decided to stop lying. "It helps people picture you and relate to you more reliably," he said. "Truth can be positively beneficial in many ways."

I asked what would happen if he found himself in a situation where it would prove *more* beneficial for him to lie. He said he would have to judge the context, but he was trying to prefer not-lying.

An Unprecedented Dilemma

For Sam, the decision to lie or tell the truth involved not morality but a social construct, to be adopted or rejected as a matter of expedience. In essence, the source of moral authority for Sam is himself, and that in a nutshell is the dilemma confronting moral philosophy in the postmodern world.

Something unprecedented in human history is brewing: a rejection of external moral sources altogether. Individuals and societies have always been im-moral to varying degrees. Individuals (never an entire society) have sometimes declared themselves amoral, professing agnosticism about ethical matters. Only recently, however, have serious thinkers entertained the notion of un-morality: that there is no such thing as morality. A trend prefigured by Friedrich Nietzsche, prophesied by Fyodor Dostoyevsky, and analyzed presciently by C.S. Lewis in *The Abolition of Man* is now coming to fruition. The very concept of

Excerpted from "Nietzsche Was Right," by Philip Yancey, *Books & Culture*, January/February 1998. Reprinted with permission from the author.

morality is undergoing a profound change, led in part by the advance guard of a new science called "evolutionary psychology."

So far, however, the pioneers of unmorality have practiced a blatant contradiction. Following in the style of Jean-Paul Sartre, who declared that meaningful communication is impossible even as he devoted his life to communicating meaningfully, the new moralists first proclaim that morality is capricious, perhaps even a joke, then

> *"If we learn our morality from nature, . . . why should not the strong exercise their 'natural rights' over the weak?"*

proceed to use moral categories to condemn their opponents. These new high priests lecture us solemnly about multiculturalism, gender equality, homophobia, and environmental degradation, all the while ignoring the fact that they have systematically destroyed any basis for judging such behavior right or wrong. The emperor so quick to discourse about fashion happens to be stark naked.

For example, George Williams wrote a landmark book in 1966 entitled *Adaptation and Natural Selection,* which portrayed all behavior as a genetically programmed expression of self-interest. Yet later, after examining some of the grosser examples of animal behavior, he concluded that "Mother Nature is a wicked old witch. . . . Natural selection really is as bad as it seems and . . . it should be neither run from nor emulated, but rather combatted."

Williams neglected to explain what allowed him, a product of pure natural selection, to levitate above nature and judge it morally bankrupt. He may understandably disapprove of animal cannibalism and rape, but on what grounds can he judge them "evil"? And how can we—or why should we—combat something programmed into our genes?

Lest I sound like a cranky middle-aged moralist, I should clarify at the beginning that to me the real question is not why modern secularists oppose traditional morality; it is on what grounds they defend *any* morality.

The Morality of the Church

> We hold these truths to be probable enough for pragmatists, that all things looking like men were evolved somehow, being endowed by heredity and environment with no equal rights but very unequal wrongs. . . Men will more and more realize that there is no meaning in democracy if there is no meaning in anything. And there is no meaning in anything if the universe has not a center of significance and an authority that is the author of our rights.
>
> —G.K. Chesterton

In a great irony, the "politically correct" movement defending the rights of women, minorities, and the environment often positions itself as an enemy of the Christian church when, in historical fact, the church has contributed the very underpinnings that make such a movement possible. Christianity brought an end to slavery, and its crusading fervor also fueled the early labor movement, women's suffrage, human-rights campaigns, and civil rights. According to Robert Bellah, "there has not been a major issue in the history of the United States on which religious bodies did not speak out, publicly and vociferously."

It was no accident that Christians pioneered in the antislavery movement, for their beliefs had a theological impetus. Both slavery and the oppression of women were based, anachronistically, on an embryonic form of Darwinism. Aristotle had observed that

> Tame animals are naturally better than wild animals, yet for all tame animals there is an advantage in being under human control, as this secures their survival. And as regards the relationship between male and female, the former is naturally superior, the latter inferior, the former rules and the latter is subject. By analogy, the same must necessarily apply to mankind as a whole. Therefore all men who differ from one another by as much as the soul differs from the body or man from a wild beast (and that is the state of those who work by using their bodies, and for whom that is the best they can do)—these people are slaves by nature, and it is better for them to be subject to this kind of control, as it is better for the other creatures I have mentioned. . . . It is clear that there are certain people who are free and certain people who are slaves by nature, and it is both to their advantage, and just, for them to be slaves. . . . From the hour of their birth, some men are marked out for subjection, others for rule.

Cross out the name *Aristotle* and read the paragraph again as the discovery of a leading evolutionary psychologist. No one is proposing the reimposition of slavery, of course—but why not? If we learn our morality from nature, and if our only rights are those we create for ourselves, why should not the strong exercise their "natural rights" over the weak?

> *"Scientists who dismantle any notion of good and evil nevertheless must fall back on those categories of judgment."*

As Alasdair MacIntyre remarks in *After Virtue,* modern protesters have not abandoned moral argument, though they have abandoned any coherent platform from which to make a moral argument. They keep using moral terminology—it is *wrong* to own slaves, rape a woman, abuse a child, despoil the environment, discriminate against homosexuals—but they have no "higher authority" to which to appeal to make their moral judgments. MacIntyre concludes,

> Hence the *utterance* of protest is characteristically addressed to those who already *share* the protestors' premises. The effects of incommensurability ensure that protestors rarely have anyone else to talk to but themselves. This is not to say that protest cannot be effective; it is to say that it cannot be *rationally* effective and that its dominant modes of expression give evidence of a certain perhaps unconscious awareness of this.

In the United States, we prefer to settle major issues on utilitarian or pragmatic grounds. But philosophers including Aristotle and David Hume argued powerfully in favor of slavery on those very grounds. Adolf Hitler pursued his genocidal policies against the Jews and "defective" persons on utilitarian grounds. Unless modern thinkers can locate a source of moral authority somewhere else than in the collective sentiments of human beings, we will always be vulnerable to dangerous swings of moral consensus.

What Makes a Person Good?

> A man who has no assured and ever-present belief in the existence of a personal God or of a future existence with retribution or reward, can have for his rule of life, as far as I can see, only to follow those impulses and instincts which are the strongest or which seem to him the best ones.

—Charles Darwin

Christina Hoff Sommers tells of a Massachusetts educator attempting to teach values-clarification to her class of sixth-graders. One day her canny students announced that they valued cheating and wanted the freedom to practice it in class. Hoist with her own petard, the teacher could only respond that since it was *her* class, she insisted on honesty; they would have to exercise their dishonesty in other places. In view of such an approach to morality, should it surprise us to learn from surveys that half of all students cheat? What restrains the other half?

What makes a person good? What is "good" anyway? Moral philosophers such as Charles Taylor and Alasdair MacIntyre argue convincingly that many people in the modern world can no longer answer that question coherently.

A friend of mine named Susan, a committed Christian, told me that her husband did not measure up and she was actively looking for other men to meet her needs for intimacy. When Susan mentioned that she rose early each day to "spend an hour with the Father," I asked, "In your meetings with the Father, do any moral issues come up that might influence this pending decision about leaving your husband?"

Susan bristled: "That sounds like the response of a white Anglo-Saxon male. The Father and I are into relationship, not morality. Relationship means being wholly supportive and standing alongside me, not judging." I gently pointed out that we all make judgments in our relationships. Had not she judged her husband incapable of meeting her needs? Susan fended off my arguments, and we moved on to more congenial topics.

> *"Psychopaths represent the group that acts most consistently to the new code of 'unmorality.'"*

Like many moderns, my friend Susan has moved the locus of morality from an external to an internal source, a change that traces back to the Romantic movement and its new celebration of the individual. In his essay "Self-Reliance," Ralph Waldo Emerson proclaimed that everyone should "Trust thyself," for divinity resides in every person. What if your intuitions are evil? Emerson did not back down: "They do not seem to me to be such; but if I am the devil's child, I will live then from the devil. No law can be sacred to me but that of my nature."

Jean-Jacques Rousseau, a grandfather of Romanticism, had followed the dictates of his heart by abandoning five infants born to his illiterate servant-mistress. Of course, one could find many such scandalous incidents before the outbreak of Romanticism. The real change was more subtle and subterranean. From Aristotle onward, the West had always perceived "the good" as an external code, neither mine nor yours. Though one could choose to break the code, it remained an external code above and beyond the reach of any individual. With Romanticism, the code moved inside so as to become radically subjective. The individual self began writing his or her own moral script.

> *"Without a belief in God or afterlife, a person can only follow those impulses and instincts that are the strongest."*

The Genetic Explanation

Nearly two centuries after the flowering of Romanticism, we are witnessing the consequences of that unmooring of the moral code. In a strange twist, whereas Augustine viewed evil as a perversion of good, modern ethicists view goodness as a manifestation of selfishness. Everything we do, including every act of nobility or altruism, serves a hidden purpose: to enhance oneself or to perpetuate genetic material. Challenged to explain Mother Teresa's behavior, sociobiologist Edward O. Wilson pointed out that she was secure in the service of Christ and in her belief in immortality; in other words, believing she would get her reward, she acted on that "selfish" basis.

Robertson McQuilkin, a college president who resigned in order to care for his Alzheimer's-afflicted wife, attended a seminar in which a researcher reported that, in her study of 47 couples facing terminal illness, she had predicted with 100 percent accuracy who would die soonest, simply by observing the relationship between husband and wife. "Love helps survival," she concluded. From there, McQuilkin went directly to another session in which an expert listed reasons why families might choose to keep an ailing family member at home rather than in a nursing facility. Noting that the reasons all boiled down to economic necessity or guilt feelings, McQuilkin asked, "What about love?" "Oh," replied the expert, "I put that under guilt."

While redefining goodness, modern society has simultaneously discarded the notion of sin. In the movie *Ironweed,* Helen, an alcoholic, informs God at a candlelit altar, "You may call them sins; I call them decisions." Increasingly, bad actions are seen as neither sins nor decisions, rather as the outworking of behavior patterns hardwired into our brains. A murderer goes free on the grounds that eating Twinkies contributed to his mental instability; a national authority excuses political consultant Dick Morris's adultery as the normal biological response to an environment of power and status.

I have already mentioned that scientists who dismantle any notion of good and evil nevertheless must fall back on those categories of judgment. This kind of moral schizophrenia expresses itself at every level of society. We must cling to some form of morality or both person and society will swirl apart. Yet individuals find themselves unable to articulate a code of morality, and even less able to keep any code. Abbie Hoffman, a radical leader in the 1960s, complained, "I've never liked guilt-tripping. I've always left the concept of sin to the Catholic Church. When I was four, my mother said, 'There's millions of people starving in China. Eat your dinner.' I said, 'Ma, name one.'" Yet this rebel against guilt trips ran a distinctively "moral" campaign against a repressive society and an unjust war.

Pathology

After interviewing average Americans to determine why they behave the way they do, Robert Bellah and his associates came up with a primary ethic of "self-fulfillment." Bellah acknowledges that most people want to be "good" even though few can articulate a reason for it. In their roles as parents, spouses, and citizens, ordinary people demonstrate qualities of sacrifice, fidelity, and altruism. They act, in Bellah's opinion, out of "habits of the heart" rooted primarily in America's Christian heritage. Remove those habits of the heart, and the true pathology of modern times comes to light.

> *"Civilization holds together when a society learns to place moral values above the human appetites for power, wealth, violence, and pleasure."*

Indeed, psychopaths represent the group that acts most consistently to the new code of "unmorality." Immune to social pressures, these deviants live out the courage of their nonconvictions.

"Character," says Robert Coles, "is how you behave when no one is looking." Coles goes on to suggest that for the conscientious, those with a highly developed moral sense, "someone is always 'looking,' even if we are as solitary as Thoreau at Walden." But for the psychopath or sociopath, the "unmoral" person, no one is ever looking. The unmoral person believes in no outside source of moral authority and inside hears only the "terrible silences of an emotionally abandoned early life or the demonic voices of a tormented childhood."

Prison interviews with two mass murderers, Jeffrey Dahmer and Ted Bundy, bear out Coles's observation. Both were asked how they could possibly do the things they did. Both replied that, at the time, they did not believe in God and felt accountable to no one. They started with petty cruelty, then moved to torture of animals and people, and then murder. Nothing internal or external stopped them from making the descent to unmorality—they felt no twinge of guilt. Ironically, both mass murderers followed to logical conclusion the principle laid down by Charles Darwin a century ago—that without a belief in God or after-life, a person can only follow those impulses and instincts that are the strongest.

We read daily in the newspapers the tragic results of those who follow their strongest impulses. Bill Moyers asked the late Joseph Campbell what results when a society no longer embraces a religion or powerful mythology. "What we've got on our hands," Campbell replied; ". . . read the *New York Times*."

Not only for psychopaths, but for everyday sinners, the practice of looking inside for moral guidance is fraught with danger. Woody Allen, a sophisticated, brilliant filmmaker, granted an interview to *Time* magazine in order to counter his wife's accusations against sexual abuse of her children and to explain his affair with his 21-year-old adopted Korean daughter. "The heart wants what it wants," said Allen. "There's no logic to those things. You meet someone and you fall in love and that's that."

Symptoms of Moral Illness

It is easy to see that the moral sense has been bred out of certain sections of the population, like the wings have been bred off certain chickens to produce more white meat on them. This is a generation of wingless chickens.

—Flannery O'Connor

What happens when an entire society becomes populated with wingless chickens? I need not dwell on the contemporary symptoms of moral illness in the United States: our rate of violent crime has quintupled in my lifetime; a third of all babies are now born out of wedlock; half of all marriages end in divorce; the richest nation on earth has a homeless population larger than the entire population of some nations. These familiar symptoms are just that, symptoms. A diagnosis would look beyond them to our loss of a teleological sense. "Can one be a saint if God does not exist? That is the only concrete problem I know of today," wrote Albert Camus in *The Fall*.

Civilization holds together when a society learns to place moral values above the human appetites for power, wealth, violence, and pleasure. Historically, it has always relied on religion to provide a source for that moral authority. In fact, according to Will and Ariel Durant, "There is no significant example in history, before our time, of a society successfully maintaining moral life without the aid of religion." They added the foreboding remark, "The greatest question of our time is not communism versus individualism, not Europe versus America, not even the East versus the West; it is whether men can live without God."

"There is no significant example in history, before our time, of a society successfully maintaining moral life without the aid of religion."

Vàclav Havel, a survivor of a civilization that tried to live without God, sees the crisis clearly:

I believe that with the loss of God, man has lost a kind of absolute and universal system of coordinates, to which he could always relate everything, chiefly himself. His world and his personality gradually began to break up into separate, incoherent fragments corresponding to different, relative, coordinates.

On moral issues—social justice, sexuality, marriage and family, definitions of life and death—society badly needs a moral tether, or "system of coordinates" in Havel's phrase. Otherwise, our laws and politics will begin to reflect the same kind of moral schizophrenia already seen in individuals. . . .

Redefining Morality

Critics of Christianity correctly point out that the church has proved an unreliable carrier of moral values. The church has indeed made mistakes, launching Crusades, censuring scientists, burning witches, trading in slaves, supporting tyrannical regimes. Yet the church also has an inbuilt potential for self-correction because it rests on a platform of transcendent moral authority. When human beings take upon themselves the Luciferian chore of redefining morality, untethered to any transcendent source, all hell breaks loose.

In Nazi Germany, and also in the Soviet Union, China, and Cambodia, the government severed morality from its roots. Nazi propagandists dismissed biblical revelation as "Jewish swindle" and emphasized instead the general revelation they observed in the natural order of creation. Vladimir Lenin ordered Russians to adopt "the Revolutionary Conscience" as opposed to their natural conscience.

> *"The church . . . rests on a platform of transcendent moral authority."*

Our century is the first in which societies have attempted to form their moral codes without reference to religion. We have had the chance to "take the world in our own hands," in Camus's phrase. Modern humanity, Camus said, "launches the essential undertaking of rebellion, which is that of replacing the reign of grace by the reign of justice." The results are in: perhaps 100 million deaths under Hitler, Joseph Stalin, Mao Tse-tung, and Pol Pot attributable to this grand new reign of justice.

Today, of course, apart from China, the threat posed by communism has disappeared. We in the West rest secure, even triumphant. Yet the bats are out of the cage. The spiritual sources that fed both Nazism and communism are still with us.

We look back with horror on the Nazi campaign to exterminate the mentally defective. But not long ago the newsletter of a California chapter of Mensa, the organization for people with high IQs, published an article proposing the elimination of undesirable citizens, including the retarded and the homeless. Modern China requires the abortion of defective fetuses, including those diagnosed with retardation, and kills "unauthorized" babies born to one-child families. And in some states in the United States, due largely to pressures from insurance companies, the incidence of Down syndrome children has dropped 60 percent; the rest are aborted before birth.

Religion Is the Basis of Morality

In his study *Morality: Religious and Secular,* Basil Mitchell argues that, since the eighteenth century, secular thinkers have attempted to make reason, not religion, the basis of morality. None has successfully found a way to establish an *absolute* value for the individual human person. Mitchell suggests that secular thinkers can establish a relative value for people, by comparing people to animals, say, or to each other; but the idea that every person has an absolute value came out of Christianity and Judaism before it and is absent from every other ancient philosophy or religion.

The Founding Fathers of the United States, apparently aware of the danger, made a valiant attempt to connect individual rights to a transcendent source. Overruling Thomas Jefferson, who had made only a vague reference to "the Laws of Nature and of Nature's God," they insisted instead on including the words "unalienable" and "endowed by their Creator." They did so in order to secure such rights in a transcendent Higher Power, so that no human power could attempt to take them away. Human dignity and worth derive from God's.

they've cheated on an exam." How does this show up in the workplace? "Twenty percent of the workers in one survey said they had lied to their employer about something important in the last year," Josephson says. "Sixty percent said they had a low level of confidence in the integrity of their corporation's internal reports, and 33 percent believed there was a 'kill the messenger syndrome' that forced them to lie and cover up. Corporations have made tremendous investments in literacy because they need workers who can read. Now they're investing in moral literacy because they also need an honest work force."

Taking the Message Public

For that reason, companies are moving more forcefully into the community. "Through their programs, corporations are taking on a new leadership role in society," says Daigneault. "They are an important influence in people's lives. They're positively reinforcing people, saying that it's okay to talk about values and ethical principles. People used to look to the government to teach values. Companies have begun to take over that role.

"Take the public schools," Daigneault continues. "There was a time when most people believed the school system's job was to educate children and to create good citizens. Then, in the 1950s and '60s, schools adopted a philosophy of 'values clarification.' Instead of telling students what to think, teachers would lead them through the process of examining values. When the big problems were gum chewing and talking in class, values clarification worked fine. These days, the big problems are rape, weapons, and drugs, and values clarification isn't as useful."

The current antidote is "character education," which teaches the basic values—honesty, respect for others—that society expects of its members. Bell Atlantic Corp., in conjunction with the Ethics Resource Center, has developed a curriculum package for character education that it is making available to school administrators nationwide. Jacquelyn B. Gates, Bell Atlantic's ethics VP, says the company got interested in public education because employees were calling its ethics hotline with concerns about their children's schools. "If people perceive that corporations have the responsibility to intervene," says Daigneault, "it's because corporations have the power."

With major corporations pushing values, one has to wonder what the larger effect on society might be. Are we headed toward, if not the Age of Aquarius, a more moral climate?

"There are hopeful signs," says Michael Josephson, "but you can't point to any social change. Ethics might be just another issue du jour, like total quality management, risk taking, and thinking outside the box. Phases and fads go through the corporate world. We trained 2,000 IRS employees, yet the IRS has no institutional memory that we were ever there. It's too early to tell what the impact of all this activity will be, but it would be a mistake to dismiss the movement."

Ethical Practices Benefit Corporations

by Stephen Butler

About the author: *Stephen Butler is the chief executive officer of KPMG Peat Marwick, a financial services firm.*

Because of the very nature of what KPMG [Peat Marwick] does and its stature as one of the Big Six [accounting firms], we have access to and knowledge of the best practices of many world-class companies. That inside look has taught me many things, not the least of which is: good ethics means good business. One way you as business leaders can protect your position is to install, enforce and re-enforce a culture and standard of ethical conduct within your organization that can't be challenged.

Ethics and Self-Interest

Now some of you may be thinking it's unusual for me to stand up here and promote higher ethical standards in corporate America, especially since I am a CEO that is strongly focused on the bottom line! Or you may be thinking that I'm doing this to infer that KPMG wears the white hats and our competitors, black ones. . . . Not so. Neither of these reasons are valid or are driving my comments today.

And I'm not a tree hugger either. I do want to be able to look myself in the mirror each morning and respect the person I see. I want to know that my 13-year-old son, John, can and does admire me, and that my mother does too.

But I want to stress at the outset that the strongest argument for raising the ethics bar boils down to self-interest. I believe that good business ethics is good for the bottom line and good for shareholder value.

As corporations, we live at the sufferance of the public. If we don't behave well, we can be regulated, we can be sued, all sorts of bad things can happen to us. And everyday, it seems, yet another company is the subject of the "wrong kind" of story in the *Wall Street Journal*. Stories about sexual harassment, environmental contamination, antitrust infractions, illegal foreign payments, fraudu-

Excerpted from "Business Ethics and Corporate Responsibility: Good for the Bottom Line," by Stephen Butler, speech given to recognize 100 Florida companies, February 28, 1997, Orlando, FL. Reprinted with permission.

lent financial reporting and race issues. Today, companies cannot afford negative publicity. Loss of confidence in an organization is the single greatest cost of unethical behavior. Once the media gets hold of that story, your customers will avoid you like the plague. An essential part of an ethics process is identifying issues that would mortify a chief executive if he were to read about them on the front page of the newspapers.

> *"Good ethics means good business."*

What it all translates into is this. We live in a time when the ill considered actions of a handful of employees can suddenly reverse years of effort to build a solid corporate name.

And I'm saying this because I really believe that corporate ethics are essential for a successful business today and the CEOs of corporate America are the only ones who can institutionalize it.

I'm not a scholar in the field of ethics, or a person uniquely qualified to explore the subject. . . . I am a businessman like most of you and by choice, a leader. And although I think the thousands of people who work for KPMG believe I lead with a degree of vision, I know I lead mostly with common sense.

Common sense dictates many of the decisions I make both large and small. However, there's a problem with common sense. What I may think is pure, unadulterated common sense, someone else may not. So if we business leaders rely on the common sense of our co-workers to act in an ethical manner, it simply won't happen as we imagine and even expect it to. We can't take ethics for granted assuming that problems only happen to the other guy.

Judging Corporate Character

People already judge the worth of my company and yours, not just by our bottom line, but by the contents of our corporate character. They judge our employees not just by their work product. Is it enough to have the cheapest shirt or the cheapest pair of pants sitting on the store shelves? Ask those companies that have been publicly flogged for supplying the competitively priced goods that we demand, that were sewn together in sweatshops or by child labor making pennies a day.

On the other hand, take a look at Johnson & Johnson—a company that is the hallmark of American corporate ethics. Their code of ethics is a part of the very fabric of the company reaching as far back as the mid '40s. In the 1980s, J&J's response to not one but two Tylenol tragedies [when bottles of Tylenol were discovered to contain lethal doses of cyanide] and its subsequent media exposure etched in the public's collective mind the reputation of Johnson & Johnson as the company to trust.

By voluntarily pulling massive amounts of at-risk product immediately off the shelf, J&J proved that its corporate decision making was driven by what was ethical, not expeditious. But were their actions good business? You judge.

Within days of the second Tylenol tragedy their stock actually climbed ten points, with analysts attributing the rise to the company's speedy and ethical crisis response. . . .

Instituting a corporate ethics program in an organization isn't a matter of religion. It isn't a spiritual issue, not even strictly a legal or regulatory issue. It's simply the right thing to do. And in the long haul, companies will and do profit from having and enforcing strong ethics programs.

But what is the definition of ethics? According to the dictionary, ethics is a system of moral principles or values.

For me, the answer is simpler. Evil people will do whatever they want one way or another. That bad people do bad things is uncontrollable. Ethics means making sure good people don't do bad things, intentionally or unintentionally. But the evidence is mounting that much of the time the employees who engage in the most damaging misconduct are basically good people who think they are doing what their company really wants. The goal of business ethics is to keep good people from lapsing, or from looking the other way.

Mixed Signals

Serious problems most typically arise when people feel incented or pressured to do things they shouldn't. One study, published by the California Management Review in January 1995, looked at the first five years after graduation and employment of 30 Harvard University MBA graduates. Twenty-nine of them said that business pressures had forced them to violate their own personal ethical standards.

People tend to do what they perceive their company, manager or supervisor wants them to do. And based on their work environment or culture, people usually decide what it takes to be successful, then go in that direction. To me that means there are a lot of mixed signals being sent. Do we want our employees to be ethical or are we signaling them to do whatever it takes to just get it done? The message is pointedly driven home to them in performance evaluations, pay raises, promotions, and not so subtle reminders that others can do their job if they "can't cut it."

> *"Good business ethics is good for the bottom line and good for shareholder value."*

At the same time they are vaguely aware of a company code of conduct that tells them to act honestly and they have also received some training.

Too often they resolve these two seemingly competing messages in favor of the business goal, because they hear that message more loudly than the ethics message. They keep their heads down and quietly do what they assume is what the company really wants them to do: just get it done, whatever it takes.

Ethics programs must be more than window dressing that creates a paper trail to cover our behinds. Our role as leaders is to set the tone at the top by ment to work together to establish an appropriate set of rules for this research. These rules will ensure the advancement of critical medical research and maintain respect for public sensibilities.

The National Institutes of Health has already developed an outline of such a system. For federally funded research, this system will prohibit the use of pluripotent stem cells that have come from "embryo farms" or from embryos purchased or sold, and will continue to ensure that human embryos are not created for research purposes. It will also continue to be illegal to use federal funds to derive pluripotent stem cells from human embryos.

• Banning federal funding for human pluripotent stem cell research will not eliminate it. Such research will proceed in private industry and in other countries. This fact prompts serious concern that the work may then be conducted in secret, without the benefit of ethical regulation or public debate as it proceeds.

• Using federal funds for human pluripotent stem cell research ensures that our best and most capable scientists will participate in this research. Without such funding, new treatments will be delayed by years, and

> *"Should we not use cells derived from donated embryos to save lives?"*

many who might otherwise have been saved will surely die or endure needless suffering.

• Federal funding is the best way to guarantee that stem cell therapies are developed with the greatest consideration of the public good. In the absence of federal funding, it is likely that stem-cell derived treatments will only be found for diseases that commercial companies determine will yield the largest profit if treated. Thus, market forces could create a situation where deadly, but less profitable, diseases are ignored.

No Other Ethical Use

• Although it is essential that we use federal funds to support pluripotent stem cell research, the stem cells themselves will be derived without using federal funds from early embryos that are destined to be discarded. In vitro fertilization treatments for childless couples often produce more embryos than can be implanted into the mother. These embryos cannot develop on their own, have only a few cells, and must either be stored in freezers indefinitely, or eventually destroyed.

There is no other ethical use for these embryos if the parents choose not to have them implanted into the mother. Even if one believes that the destruction of these embryos is a tragedy, should we not allow the parents the right to make the decision to donate them for pluripotent stem cell derivation and stem cell research so that many other people might live? Should we not use cells derived from donated embryos to save lives, just as we do after an auto accident by using the organs of those who tragically died?

Ethics

• Balancing the ethical objections of some to pluripotent stem cell research are the serious ethical implications of not proceeding. Can we justify turning our backs on our children, parents and friends who will suffer and die if we do not find suitable cures? Ethically validated pluripotent stem cell research provides new hope for these people.

In the past few years, Congress has wisely and dramatically increased federal funding for biomedical research. We must ensure that these funds are used for the best and most promising medical research.

Ethics, scientific opportunity and medical need can surely be balanced. Ask Walter Payton or my friend Doug if you're still not sure.

Allowing the Sale of Human Organs Could Be Ethical

by Pete du Pont

About the author: *Formerly the governor of Delaware, Pete du Pont is the policy chairman for the National Center for Policy Analysis, a public policy research institute headquartered in Dallas, Texas.*

There are currently about 45,000 people waiting for a human organ transplant. About 3,000 of them will die on that waiting list because a suitable transplant organ will not become available in time.

The short supply of organs has recently led to some overt attempts to ration them in a way that would be more beneficial to society. For example, the United Network for Organ Sharing has altered its guidelines for those needing a liver transplant so that those with acute liver problems get priority. Those with a chronic liver condition like hepatitis or cirrhosis (which could be the result of alcohol abuse) cannot rise above the second level in priority status.

The legislature in the state of Washington recently passed a measure—which the governor vetoed for being too vague—that would prohibit those on Death Row from receiving "lifesaving health care procedures" such as an organ transplant.

Now the Cleveland Clinic is being accused of removing organs before some patients are legally dead.

Instead of looking for new ways to ration organs or take them prematurely, we should ask how we can increase the supply of organs so that doctors are not forced to decide who lives and who dies.

Compensating Donors

The answer is to compensate donors for their organs. Unfortunately, doing so is currently against the law. That's because the National Organ Transplant Act (1984) prohibits "any person to knowingly acquire, receive or otherwise trans-

Reprinted from "Market Card for Organ Donors?" by Pete du Pont, *The Washington Times,* October 2, 1997. Reprinted with permission from the author.

fer any human organ for valuable consideration for use in human transplantation." As a result, altruism is the only legal motive for individuals or their surrogates to donate their organs.

But while altruism is a noble motive, it is seldom a compelling one. Economic theory clearly recognizes that when demand for a good or service is high, its price will increase until the supply and demand reach an equilibrium. If the price is prohibited from rising, a shortage will occur because people will not provide a product when the price is too low. Thus, permitting donors to receive some type of compensation for their organs would help alleviate our organ-shortage problem.

Opponents of a market for organs immediately conjure up images of strange people selling off body parts. But a market for organs could develop in a number of ways: Some would be more open and direct, while others might be indirect and incorporate the concerns of some of those who oppose compensation.

We could, for example, permit a donor pool. Dr. Robert M. Sade, a surgeon and professor of medicine at the Medical University of South Carolina, and his colleagues have proposed creating an in-kind market for organs. Every adult would be given the option of joining the Transplant Recipient and Donor Organization. Membership would require permission to have your organs removed at death, and only those joining would be permitted to receive a transplanted organ. Those who chose not to join would be electing for standard medical care, short of transplantation. Thus, the only way to receive an organ while living would be to have given permission to have your organs taken at death.

> **"Permitting donors to receive some type of compensation for their organs would help alleviate our organ-shortage problem."**

Permit people to receive after-death compensation. A person wanting to become an organ donor would simply contract with an organ-donor organization, which would compensate the deceased's estate for each organ successfully harvested. The compensation could be in a variety of forms. A hospital or organ-donor network might pay part or all of a donor's burial expenses, for example. Such a provision might encourage lower-income people who could not afford life insurance to sign up for the program as a way to provide for their funeral costs. (A similar provision has been supported by an article in the *Journal of the American Medical Association.*)

Or contribute funds to the donor's designated charity—a hospital, university or social services agency. Let people sell whatever they want, when they want. The most open and market-oriented approach would be to let anyone who wanted to sell one or more organs do so. Thus, if someone needed a kidney and was willing to pay for one, a compatible donor could provide the recipient with a kidney for the market-set price.

ture removal," i.e., removing the vital organs of a person who is not yet dead.

To deal with these problems, the medical community has developed strict criteria for defining what is called "brain death." These criteria are extremely detailed and, until now, very much biased toward presuming that life continues: there is virtually no possibility that a person who is actually still living will be proclaimed dead. For example, someone who has been comatose for years, and whose responsiveness is

> *"An anencephalic baby is still a baby after all."*

limited to a few primitive reflexes, will still not qualify as "brain dead" by these criteria. Neither will an anencephalic baby; that is, a baby born with no cerebral cortex but with enough brain matter to permit primitive reflexes. And that brings us to the latest development in the ethics of transplantation.

Consider the following. Of all the children whose lives could be saved by an organ transplant, half die because of a shortage of donated organs. On the other hand, anencephalic babies, who are born with almost no brain but are otherwise physically normal, can only survive a few days after birth. On the surface, it seems like an almost perfect match: the organs of a baby who cannot live can be used to rescue another child who must otherwise die. That, at least, is how it looked to physicians at Loma Linda University in 1987, when they set up a special program designed to salvage the organs of anencephalic babies for transplantation. However, in eight months of operation the program failed to salvage even one viable organ. Why? Simply because these babies were not "brain dead" at birth: impaired as they were, they retained enough brain function to fail the criteria for death. By the time these babies finally did die, their organs had suffered severe damage and were no longer usable.

The physicians and nurses at Loma Linda accepted their defeat, some of them with considerable relief. An anencephalic baby is still a *baby* after all, and the act of inflicting intensive care on a dying infant simply in order to be able to harvest its organs after death began to take an emotional toll on the staff.

The "Baby Theresa" Case

There are some, however, who are not so willing to relinquish this potential source of donor organs. In 1992 the Florida State Supreme Court heard the "Baby Theresa" case. In this case the parents, backed by the American Civil Liberties Union (ACLU), requested that their anencephalic baby be declared dead at birth, even though she did not meet the accepted criteria for brain death, so that her heart could be transplanted into another child. One can only guess what the parents' motives and feelings were. Perhaps they were trying to assuage guilt feelings or offer themselves comfort by trying to bring some good out of a tragic situation. Perhaps they were able, by some exercise of self-hypnosis, to avoid realizing what would actually be done to their baby: that she would be taken to an operating room, and there—even though she was able to breathe, kick, and cry—her heart would be removed for use as a "donor organ."

The reasoning of the ACLU in this case was chilling. They noted "the inconsistency of permitting the termination of pregnancies up to the moment of birth" while at the same time "prohibiting the donation of organs just after birth." As they put it, "There is absolutely no morally significant change in the fetus between the moments immediately preceding and following birth." Note that exactly the same argument used by the pro-life movement for years in defending the unborn is now being used by the ACLU to justify infanticide.

It is not hard to see where this reasoning leads. Though the ACLU denies that its position "serves as a springboard to institutional murder," it clearly does just that. The reasoning used to justify declaring anencephalic babies "dead" at birth can be applied with equal logic to any other baby whose deformities might have moved its parents to abort it, had they but known of them. In fact, this reasoning really strips all newborns of any protection. If abortion on demand "up to the very moment of birth" is morally acceptable, as the ACLU asserts, why not infanticide on demand? And why stop at infants? There are millions of retarded children and adults whose lives are below the high standards of the social engineers. Why not declare them dead as well? At a stroke, the organ shortage could be solved.

> *"Even though she was able to breathe, kick, and cry—her heart would be removed for use as a 'donor organ.'"*

Fortunately, the Florida Supreme Court had the uncommon (these days) good sense to reject the ACLU's arguments. Baby Theresa was allowed to live out her short life without being terminated for some "higher good." But it was too much to hope that the notion of harvesting organs from handicapped infants would die with her.

In the summer of 1994, no less an authority than the American Medical Association (AMA) Council on Ethical and Judicial Affairs declared that it is "ethically permissible" for anencephalic infants to be used as donors while still alive. In its opinion, the Council admitted that it is normally preferable for an organ donor to be dead before removing vital organs, but made an exception in the case of anencephalics for two main reasons: first, "because of the great need for children's organs," and second, because anencephalics "have never experienced, and will never experience, consciousness." Or, as one supporter of the decision bluntly put it, "The quality of life for this child is so low it would be ethically justifiable to sacrifice its life by a few days to save the life of another person."

Extending the Reasoning to Others

Such reasoning cannot be confined to the narrow case of anencephalics. Due to improvements in prenatal care the incidence of anencephaly has declined steadily, so that fewer than one hundred babies with anencephaly are likely to be born in the United States each year, and many of them are born with such serious organ defects that they would be excluded as organ donors. Clearly, anencephalics alone would not begin to address the "great need for children's organs" that the Council cited in justifying its decision.

The Council's decision must be seen for what it is—the thin edge of the wedge. Using the dual arguments of "no possibility of consciousness" and "poor quality of life," it will not be difficult to extend the Council's reasoning widely. What about children and adults in a "persistent vegetative state"? If in the judgment of the medical experts such people no longer have the possibility of consciousness, what ethical obstacle remains to removing their vital organs? What about the profoundly retarded who, as all compassionate social planners will agree, have a "low quality of life"? What about a child with third-degree burns over 90 percent of his body? He has no chance of survival, and an obviously low quality of life, yet his heart is beating strongly—a heart that another child could use. Why not end the needless suffering of one child, and give the gift of life to another through one painless and humane operation?

"This reasoning really strips all newborns of any protection."

Unthinkable? Think again. Think first of everything that was unthinkable thirty years ago and is now commonplace: abortion on demand, the growing acceptance of euthanasia, genetic engineering, cloning, and so on. Think of the unthinkable Holocaust. The ideas behind that horror originated not with the Nazis but with the "humane" social scientists of Germany's finest universities. Then think of the combined resources of the AMA and the ACLU turned against the Baby Theresas of our society. We must anticipate the unthinkable, or the unthinkable will become routine.

Chapter 4

How Can Ethical Behavior Be Taught?

mates, who had been taught that "all knowledge is a social construct," were doubtful that the Holocaust ever occurred. One of her classmates said, "Although the Holocaust may not have happened, it's a perfectly reasonable conceptual hallucination."

A creative writing teacher at Pasadena City College wrote an article in the *Chronicle of Higher Education* about what it is like to teach Shirley Jackson's famous short story "The Lottery" to today's college students. It is a tale of a small farming community that seems normal in every way, with people who are hardworking and friendly. As the plot progresses, however, the reader learns this village carries out an annual lottery in which the loser is stoned to death.

It is a shocking lesson about primitive rituals in a modern American setting. In the past, most students had understood "The Lottery" to be a warning about the dangers of mindless conformity, but now they merely think it is "Neat!" or "Cool!" They will not go out on a limb and take a stand against human sacrifice.

It was not always thus. When Thomas Jefferson wrote that all men have the right to life, liberty, and the pursuit of happiness, he did not say, "At least that is my opinion." He declared it as an objective truth. When suffragette Elizabeth Cady Stanton "amended" the Declaration of Independence by changing the phrase "all men" to "all men and women," she was not merely giving an opinion; she was insisting that females are endowed with the same rights and entitlements as males.

> **"I often meet students incapable of making even one single confident moral judgment."**

The assertions of Jefferson and Stanton were made in the same spirit—as self-evident truths, not personal judgments. Today's young people enjoy the fruits of the battles fought by such leaders, but they are not being given the intellectual and moral training to argue for and justify truth. In fact, the kind of education they are getting systematically is undermining their common sense about what is true and right.

Let me be concrete and specific: Men and women died courageously fighting the Nazis. They included American and Allied soldiers, as well as resistance fighters. Because brave people took risks to do what was right and necessary, Germany eventually was defeated. Today, with the assault on objective truth, many college students find themselves unable to say *why* the U.S. was on the right side in that war. Some even doubt that America *was* in the right. They are not even sure the salient events of World War II ever took place. They simply lack confidence in the objectivity of history.

Too many young people are morally confused, ill-informed, and adrift. This confusion gets worse, rather than better, once they go to college. If they are attending an elite school, they actually can lose their common sense and become clever and adroit intellectuals in the worst sense. Author George Orwell reputedly said, "Some ideas are so absurd that only an intellectual could believe them." The students of such intellectuals are in the same boat. Orwell did not know about the tenured radicals of the 1990s, but he was presciently aware that they were on the way.

The problem is not that young people are ignorant, distrustful, cruel, or treacherous. It is not that they are moral skeptics. They just talk that way. To put it bluntly, they are conceptually clueless. Students are suffering from "cognitive moral confusion."

The Great Relearning

What is to be done? How can their knowledge and understanding of moral history be improved? How can their confidence in the great moral ideals be restored? How can they be helped to become morally articulate, morally literate, and morally self-confident?

In the late 1960s, a group of hippies living in the Haight-Ashbury District of San Francisco decided that hygiene was a middle-class hang-up they could do without. So, they decided to live without it. Baths and showers, while not actually banned, were frowned upon. Essayist and novelist Tom Wolfe was intrigued by these hippies, who, he said, "sought nothing less than to sweep aside all codes and restraints of the past and start out from zero."

Before long, the hippies' aversion to modern hygiene had consequences that were as unpleasant as they were unforeseen. Wolfe describes them: "At the Haight-Ashbury Free Clinic there were doctors who were treating diseases no living doctor had ever encountered before, diseases that had disappeared so long ago they had never even picked up Latin names, such as the mange, the grunge, the itch, the twitch, the thrush, the scroff, the rot." The itching and the manginess eventually began to vex the hippies, leading them to seek help from the local free clinics. Step by step, they had to rediscover for themselves the rudiments of modern hygiene. Wolfe refers to this as the "Great Relearning."

The Great Relearning is what has to happen whenever earnest reformers extirpate too much. When, "starting from zero," they jettison basic social practices and institutions, abandon common routines, and defy common sense, reason, conventional wisdom—and, sometimes, sanity itself.

This was seen with the most politically extreme experiments of the 20th century—Marxism, Maoism, and fascism. Each movement had its share of zealots and social engineers who believed in starting from zero.

> *"The kind of education [students] are getting systematically is undermining their common sense about what is true and right."*

They had faith in a new order and ruthlessly cast aside traditional arrangements. Among the unforeseen consequences were mass suffering and genocide. Russians and Eastern Europeans are beginning their own Great Relearning. They now realize, to their dismay, that starting from zero is a calamity and that the structural damage wrought by the political zealots has handicapped their societies for decades to come. They are learning that it is far easier to tear apart a social fabric than to piece one together again.

America, too, has had its share of revolutionary developments—not so much political as moral. We are living through a great experiment in "moral deregulation," an experiment whose first principle seems to be: "Conventional morality is oppressive." What is right is what works for us. We question everything. We casually, even gleefully, throw out old-fashioned

> *"We must encourage and honor colleges that accept the responsibility of providing a classical moral education for their students."*

customs and practices. Writer Oscar Wilde once said, "I can resist everything except temptation." Many in the 1960s generation made succumbing to temptation and license their philosophy of life.

We jokingly call looters "non-traditional shoppers." Killers are described as "morally challenged"—again jokingly, but the truth behind the jests is that moral deregulation is the order of the day. We poke fun at our own society for its lack of moral clarity. In our own way, we are as down and out as those hippies knocking at the door of the free clinic.

Moral Conservationism

We need our own Great Relearning. Let me propose a few ideas on how we might carry out this relearning. The first, which could be called "moral conservationism," is based on this premise: We are born into a moral environment just as we are born into a natural environment. Just as there are basic environmental necessities—clean air, safe food, and fresh water—there are basic moral necessities. What is a society without civility, honesty, consideration, and self-discipline? Without a population educated to be civil, considerate, and respectful of one another, what will we end up with? The answer is, not much. For as long as philosophers and theologians have written about ethics, they have stressed the moral basics. We live in a moral environment. We must respect and protect it. We must acquaint our children with it. We must make them aware it is precious and fragile.

My suggestions for specific reforms are far from revolutionary and, indeed, some are pretty obvious. They are commonsense ideas, but we live in an age when common sense is increasingly hard to come by.

We must encourage and honor colleges that accept the responsibility of providing a classical moral education for their students. The last few decades of the 20th century have seen a steady erosion of knowledge and a steady increase in moral relativism. This is partly due to the diffidence of many teachers confused by all the talk about pluralism. Such teachers actually believe that it is wrong to "indoctrinate" our children in our own culture and moral tradition.

Of course, there are pressing moral issues around which there is no consensus. In a modern pluralistic society, there are arguments about all sorts of things. This is understandable. Moral dilemmas arise in every generation. Nevertheless, humanity long ago achieved consensus on many basic moral questions. Cheating, cowardice, and cruelty are wrong. As one pundit put it, "The Ten Commandments are not the Ten Highly Tentative Suggestions."

Teaching the Classics

While it is true that we must debate controversial issues, we must not forget there exists a core of noncontroversial ethical issues that were settled a long time ago. Teachers must make students aware there is a standard of ethical ideals that all civilizations worthy of the name have discovered. They must be encouraged to read the Bible, Aristotle's *Ethics,* William Shakespeare's *King Lear,* the Koran, and the *Analects* of Confucius. When they read almost any great work, they will encounter these basic moral values: integrity, respect for human life, self-control, honesty, courage, and self-sacrifice. All the world's major religions proffer some version of the Golden Rule, if only in its negative form: Do not do unto others as you would not have them do unto you.

The literary classics must be taught. The great books and great ideas must be brought back into the core of the curriculum. The best of political and cultural heritage must be transmitted. Author Franz Kafka once said that a great work of literature melts the "frozen sea within us." There are any number of works of art and philosophy that have the same effect.

> *"When [students] read almost any great work, they will encounter . . . basic moral values."*

American children have a right to their moral heritage. They should know the Bible. They should be familiar with the moral truths in the tragedies of Shakespeare and the political ideas of Jefferson, James Madison, and Abraham Lincoln. They should be exposed to the exquisite moral sensibility in the novels of Jane Austen, George Eliot, and Mark Twain, to mention some of my favorites. These great works are their birthright.

This is not to say that a good literary, artistic, and philosophical education suffices to create ethical human beings, nor to suggest that teaching the classics is all that is needed to repair the moral ozone. What is known is that we can not, in good conscience, allow America's children to remain morally illiterate. All healthy societies pass along their moral and cultural traditions to their children.

Support American Culture

This suggests another basic reform. Teachers, professors, and other social critics should be encouraged to moderate their attacks on our culture and its institutions. They should be encouraged to treat great literary works as literature and not as reactionary political tracts. In many classrooms today, students are encouraged to "uncover" the allegedly racist, sexist, and elitist elements in the great books.

Meanwhile, pundits, social critics, radical feminists, and other intellectuals on the cultural left never seem to tire of running down our society and its institutions. We are overrun by determined advocacy groups that overstate the weaknesses of our society and show very little appreciation for its merits and strengths.

> *"The great books and great ideas must be brought back into the core of the curriculum."*

I urge those professors and teachers who use their classrooms to disparage America to consider the possibility that they are doing more harm than good. Their goal may be to create sensitive, critical citizens, but what they actually are doing is producing confusion and cynicism. Their goal may be to improve students' awareness of the plight of exploited peoples, but they are producing individuals capable of doubting that the Holocaust actually took place and incapable of articulating moral objections to human sacrifice.

In my opinion, we are not unlike those confused, scrofulous hippies of the late 1960s who finally showed up at the doors of the free clinics in Haight-Ashbury to get their dose of traditional medicine. I hope we have the good sense to follow their example. We need to take an active stand against the divisive unlearning that is corrupting the integrity of our society.

Writer William Butler Yeats talked of the "center" and warned that it is not holding. Others talk of the threats to our social fabric and tradition. Nevertheless, we remain a sound society. We know how to dispel the moral confusion and get back our bearings and confidence. We have traditions and institutions of proven strength and efficacy, and we still are strong.

A Great Heritage of Ethics

We need to bring back the great books and the great ideas. We need to transmit the best of our political and cultural heritage. We need to refrain from cynical attacks against our traditions and institutions. We need to expose the folly of all the schemes for starting from zero. We need to teach our young people to understand, respect, and protect the institutions that protect us and preserve our free and democratic society.

If we do, when we engage in the Great Relearning that so badly is needed today, we will find that the lives of our morally enlightened children will be saner, safer, more dignified, and more humane.

Children Can Learn Ethics Through Hunting

by Michael Pearce

About the author: *A freelance writer based in Kansas, Michael Pearce contributes frequently to* Outdoor Life, Field and Stream, *and other hunting magazines. He is the author of three books about hunting and shooting.*

I talked with a boyhood friend a while back, a guy with whom I'd shared bass ponds and bobwhite hunts years ago. As is usual for thirtysomething parents, talk eventually turned to our children.

Spending Time with Kids

Like many parents, he was confused and concerned about his two teenagers. The word coming from school wasn't good, nor were relationships around the house. "Even when we're together, we're not really *together*," he said, admitting he was worried about the kids' lack of commitment, responsibility and respect. He eventually got around to the old cliché: "Kids these days. . . ."

When his complaining turned into pensive silence, I asked him a question for which I already knew the answer. "Are you getting into the field much these days?"

"No," he replied. "I've always wanted to get the boys out hunting, but I just haven't had the time." In that response, he summed up one of the reasons so many "kids these days" act the way they do. Much of the problem is *"parents these days."*

Whether it's because they're trying to run a household on their own or hustling to maintain a standard of living their parents never dreamed of, too many people spend far too little time with their children. The results are often attention-starved girls who end up mothers before they're out of their teens and latchkey kids with such low self-esteem they cave in to the slightest peer pressure.

For years, experts have said that time spent together doing anything, even simply working around the house, can strengthen family bonds and provide some direction. But I'm convinced that, when it comes to teaching lessons that

GREG: I just want you to be on your best behavior. Kate gets home any minute.

SYLVIA: Who's Kate?

GREG: My wife. O.K.?

SYLVIA: O.K. But you don't have to hit.

GREG: Then I won't. Ever again. I promise.

SYLVIA: O.K.

(He reads. Sylvia sits looking at him. Finally.)

SYLVIA: I love you.

GREG: You do?

SYLVIA: I really do.

GREG: I think you do.

SYLVIA: Even when you hit me, I love you.

GREG: Thank you, Sylvia.

SYLVIA: *(Getting up.)* I think you're God, if you want to know.

GREG: No, now sit.

SYLVIA: But I think you're God.

GREG: No, now stay, Sylvia. Stay. And sit.

SYLVIA: I want to sit near you.

GREG: Well all right.

SYLVIA: Nearer, my God, to thee.

GREG: O.K. As long as you sit.

(Sylvia settles at his feet.)

GREG: Good girl. Now let me read the paper.

(He reads. She looks at him adoringly for another long time.)

SYLVIA: You saved my life.

GREG: I guess I did.

SYLVIA: You did. You saved my goddamn *life*. I never would have survived out there on my own.

GREG: I did what anyone would do, Sylvia.

SYLVIA: Oh no. Someone else might have ignored me. Or shooed me away. Or even turned me in. Not you. You welcomed me with open arms. I really appreciate that.

GREG: Thanks, Sylvia.

SYLVIA: I hardly knew where to turn. I was beginning to panic. I thought my days were numbered. Then there you were.

GREG: There I was, all right.

SYLVIA: I felt some immediate connection. Didn't you?

GREG: I did, actually.

SYLVIA: I feel it now.

GREG: So do I. *(Puts down his paper; looks at her.)* I do, Sylvia. *(He scratches her ears.)* You're a good girl, Sylvia. I'll try to give you a good home.

SYLVIA: Thanks, Greg. And I'll try to show my appreciation.

(He returns to his paper. She sits staring at him adoringly, her chin on the arm of the chair. She sneezes. He smiles at her. Then suddenly she jumps to her feet.)

SYLVIA: Hey!

GREG: What's the matter?

SYLVIA: *(Looking off.)* Hey! Hey! Hey!

GREG: What? *(He listens.)* Oh, that. That's the door. That's just Kate. Home from work.

SYLVIA: Hey! Hey!

GREG: Stop barking, Sylvia! She's a teacher. She likes an orderly classroom. Now show her you can be a good girl.

SYLVIA: *(Unable to control herself.)* Hey! Hey! Hey! Hey!

GREG: No, now quiet, Sylvia! Quiet down! Be a good, quiet girl.

KATE: *(Calling from off.)* Hello!

SYLVIA: Hey! Hey!

GREG: PLEASE, Sylvia. Please. Make a good first impression.

(Kate comes on, brisk, well-dressed, carrying a large tote bag.)

KATE: Am I crazy? I thought I heard a— *(Sees Sylvia.)* Dog.

GREG: This is Sylvia, Kate.

SYLVIA: *(Approaching Kate.)* Hi.

GREG: Sylvia, this is Kate.

KATE: What's going on, Greg?

SYLVIA: *(Walking around Kate, looking her over.)* Hi. I like you. I think I like you. Hi. *(Gives Kate a tentative kiss.)*

KATE: *(Brushing her off.)* Stop that. Go away! *(To Greg.)* Greg, what is this?

GREG: Now Kate…Sit, Sylvia.

SYLVIA: I was just trying to—

GREG: I said SIT.

(Sylvia sits immediately.)

SYLVIA: See?

GREG: Good girl. *(To Kate.)* Isn't she a good girl?

KATE: What's the story, Greg?

GREG: I found her in the park.

KATE: The park?

GREG: I was sitting in the park, and she jumped right into my lap.

KATE: Back up, please. You were *sitting?* In the *park?* When were you sitting in the park?

GREG: This afternoon. I took a break from the office. *(Pause.)* I had another fight with Harold. *(Pause.)* So I went to the park to cool off.

KATE: Oh Greg.

GREG: I was just sitting there. And up came Sylvia.

SYLVIA: *(Going to him.)* I love you.

GREG: I know you do, Sylvia. But sit.

SYLVIA: *(Sitting by him.)* Gladly, Greg.

KATE: Tell me another, Greg.

GREG: It's true.

KATE: You called to her.

GREG: I did not.

KATE: *(Crossing to her desk.)* You whistled. Beckoned. Something. You're always doing that with dogs.

GREG: I didn't this time, Kate. Actually I was asleep. I was dozing in the sun. And suddenly: Sylvia. Right, Sylvia?

SYLVIA: Right. Right. Exactly.

(Pause. Kate looks at Sylvia.)

KATE: Sylvia?

GREG: Sylvia.

KATE: Why *Sylvia?*

GREG: The name was on her tag. *(Showing her.)* See? "Sylvia."

KATE: What else is on her tag?

GREG: Nothing. Look. Just "Sylvia." She was lost and abandoned, Kate.

KATE: *(Skeptically.)* Sylvia...

SYLVIA: *(Waving to her.)* Hi, Kate.

GREG: See? She knows. She answers to it, don't you, Sylvia?

SYLVIA: I do! I definitely do!

KATE: What a name for a dog! Sylvia.

GREG: No, it fits. I looked it up. It means "She of the woods."

(Sylvia is now scratching vigorously.)

KATE: She of the woods has fleas.

GREG: I'll deal with that. I'll get her all checked out.

KATE: Why, Greg?

GREG: To deal with the fleas.

KATE: No, I mean why a dog, darling?

GREG: Why not?

KATE: In the *city,* Greg?

GREG: I like dogs.

KATE: I know, sweetheart. But here? Now? With the kids gone?

GREG: I love dogs.

SYLVIA: *(Going to him.)* I love *you.*

GREG: See? She knows that. She sensed it immediately. She latched right on.

KATE: I'm latching right off, Greg.

GREG: What do you mean?

KATE: Sweetheart, I'm exercising a veto. I'm saying no to Sylvia.

GREG: No?

KATE: N period. O period. Not in New York. Not at this stage of our lives. No.

GREG: Katie…

KATE: You work all day, *I* work all day. We go out a lot.

SYLVIA: *(Jumping up.)* "Out"? Did I hear "out"?

KATE: We're going out tonight, as a matter of fact.

SYLVIA: I love that word "out."

GREG: Tonight?

KATE: The Waldmans have tickets to a chamber music concert. So we're meeting for dinner, and going to that. Remember?

GREG: Oh right.

KATE: And tomorrow night we have our Spanish lessons, and Saturday we're going to the Knicks game with the Kramers…So no, Greg. No Sylvia. There's no need.

GREG: *I* have a need.

KATE: What need?

GREG: I'm not sure. But I have it.

KATE: Oh Greg.

GREG: It's a definite need.

KATE: Oh Greg.

GREG: If I could *explain* it, Kate, if I could put it neatly into words, then it wouldn't be so much of a need.

SYLVIA: I love you, Greg.

GREG: And she needs me.

SYLVIA: When do we eat?

KATE: She needs anyone who'll give her a meal.

GREG: No, it's more than that. Much more. We've bonded, Kate.

KATE: Ooo. Ouch. That's an overworked word, Greg.

GREG: I really want her, Kate.

KATE: And I really don't. So what do we do?

GREG: I don't know.

SYLVIA: *(To herself.)* I hate situations like this. I've been caught in the middle before, and I just hate it.

KATE: *(Looking at Sylvia.)* What is she? A mutt?

GREG: I think she's part Lab.

KATE: She's a mutt.

GREG: She's got a Lab's disposition. She likes everybody, don't you, Sylvia?

SYLVIA: I do. Everybody. My aim in life is to please.

GREG: I also think she may be part poodle.

SYLVIA: *(Assuming a saucy position.) Mais oui, Monsieur.* Ooo la la.

KATE: She's not the most beautiful thing I've ever seen, Greg. *(She goes out.)*

GREG: *(Calling after her.)* That's what I like about her. *(To Sylvia.)* You've got hybrid vigor, don't you, Sylvia? You are multicultural.

SYLVIA: You better believe it.

GREG: *(Calling to Kate.)* Think of her as an American, Kate! *(To Sylvia.) Canus Americanus,* that's Sylvia.

SYLVIA: I pledge allegiance. *(Brooklyn accent.)* I solemnly swear.

KATE: *(From within.)* Is she house-trained?

GREG: I think so.

KATE: *(From within.)* You *think* so?

GREG: Are you house-trained, Sylvia?

SYLVIA: *(Uneasily.)* Oh yes. Definitely. Absolutely. No question.

KATE: *(From within.)* She probably isn't.

GREG: She was a good girl walking home, weren't you, Sylvia? You were a very good girl.

SYLVIA: *(Rolling around.)* Yes I was. I was very good.

GREG: We were a very good girl. Twice. Weren't we?

(Kate returns with two drinks, sees this display.)

KATE: I may puke, Greg.

GREG: Oh look, sweetheart. Give her a chance. Poor lost soul. •

KATE: Seems to me someone else around here is behaving like a poor lost soul.

GREG: All the more reason, sweetheart. Maybe that's the need.

(The telephone rings.)

KATE: I'll get it. *(She answers.)* Oh yes, Harold. He's right here. *(Hands over receiver.)* He wants to talk.

GREG: I don't feel like talking.

KATE: He's your *boss,* for God's sake!

GREG: I'll take it in the other room. *(Starts off.)*

KATE: He sounded a little mad, Greg.

GREG: Yes well I'm mad, too. The guy thinks he owns me.

KATE: I hope you apologize.

GREG: For what?

KATE: For leaving work! In the middle of the day!

GREG: It's the best thing I've done in years.

KATE: Oh yes? Why?

GREG: It got me Sylvia.

KATE: Oh come on!

(He goes; Kate goes to her desk. She and Sylvia eye each other.)

SYLVIA: *(Finally.)* Hi.

(Kate sits at her desk, takes books and a notebook out of her bag, begins to work.)

SYLVIA: I said Hi.

KATE: *(Working.)* I'm busy, Sylvia.

(Sylvia goes to her, nudges her.)

SYLVIA: Hello, Kate.

KATE: Go away, Sylvia.

SYLVIA: I'm just trying to make friends.

KATE: Don't bother me, please. I'm trying to prepare my fall curriculum.

SYLVIA: You don't like me, do you?

KATE: *(Working.)* It's not a question of that.

SYLVIA: You don't like dogs.

KATE: I like them when they belong to other people.

SYLVIA: You're prejudiced.

KATE: Not at all.

SYLVIA: I think you're prejudiced against dogs!

KATE: *(Putting down her work.)* I am not prejudiced, Sylvia. When I was a girl, I read the Albert Payson Terhune dog books cover to cover. I watched *Lassie* on television. I'm a huge fan of *One Hundred and One Dalmatians*. When we lived in the suburbs, when the children were around, we had several dogs, and guess who ended up feeding the damn things. But I don't want a dog *now*, Sylvia. That is the point. Our last child has gone off to college, and we have moved into town, and the dog phase of my life is definitely over. I've gotten my Master's degree, Sylvia, and I have a very challenging teaching job, and frankly I don't want to worry about animals. So if you'll excuse me, I will return to the daunting task of planning how to teach Shakespeare in the inner-city junior high school. *(She returns to her work.)*

SYLVIA: O.K. Fine. No problem. *(She goes to the couch.)* I'll just stay out of your
hair. *(She steps onto the couch, turns around once or twice, then settles on it.)*
KATE: *(Looking up.)* Off, Sylvia!
SYLVIA: You speaking to me?
KATE: I said off that couch! Right now!
SYLVIA: I'm just relaxing. Can't I even relax?
(Kate leaves her desk, pulls Sylvia off the couch.)
KATE: Now off! And stay off.
SYLVIA: Easy! Take it easy!…Jesus!
KATE: I'm sorry, but you've got to learn. *(She returns to her work.)*
(Pause.)
SYLVIA: *(Sitting grumpily on the floor.)* I've sat on couches before, you know.
KATE: *(Working.)* What?
SYLVIA: I said I've sat on couches before. I've sat on plenty of couches.
KATE: Well you can't sit on this one.
SYLVIA: Hoity-toity to you.
KATE: Quiet. I'm working.
SYLVIA: *(Getting up; easing onto the chair.)* Can I at least sit on a chair?
KATE: No, Sylvia. Off!
SYLVIA: *(Slumping again onto the floor.)* Shit. Piss. Fuck.
KATE: *(Putting down her pencil.)* This is not going to work, Sylvia.
SYLVIA: What do you mean?
KATE: I'm afraid you'll have to go to the pound.
SYLVIA: Hey, I'm sitting, aren't I? I'm sitting on the floor. Look how quickly I sat.
KATE: Still, you've got to go.
SYLVIA: O.K. I get the picture. I'll avoid the furniture. I'm not dumb.
KATE: No, I'm sorry, Sylvia. You're going to the pound. I'm sure someone will
come along and give you a nice home.
SYLVIA: I've got a nice home right here.
KATE: No, now listen, Sylvia. It doesn't make sense. Nobody's around all day
long. You'd be bored out of your mind, stuck in this apartment.
SYLVIA: I don't mind. I'll sleep. I'll chew things.
KATE: That's just the trouble.
SYLVIA: All right. I *won't* chew things. Just show me the rules and I'll follow
them, I swear.
KATE: We go out a lot, Sylvia. We visit friends in the country on weekends.
We see the kids at college.
SYLVIA: I'll come, too!

KATE: *(Crossing to her.)* No, I don't want that. I want my freedom, Sylvia. I want freedom from dogs. Now you'll be much happier somewhere else.

SYLVIA: In the *pound?*

KATE: Well not the *pound,* really, Sylvia. I shouldn't have said the pound. We'll give you to…what is it? The Animal Rescue League. Or the Humane Society.

SYLVIA: They suck.

KATE: Now, now.

SYLVIA: They *suck!* You have no idea what they do.

KATE: Well I'm sure they make every effort to—

SYLVIA: Have you ever been there? Have you ever bothered to check them out?

KATE: No, but—

SYLVIA: The rows of cages. The shitty food.

KATE: Oh now.

SYLVIA: The time limit.

KATE: The time limit?

SYLVIA: They all have time limits. They don't broadcast it, but they do. If someone doesn't bail you out, normally within five working days, then they put you to sleep.

KATE: Sylvia…

SYLVIA: They do! They kill you! Listen. It's a tough world out there, lady. I know. I've been there. *(Nuzzling her.)* That's why I want to be here.

KATE: Well you can't, Sylvia. I'm terribly sorry but I really have to put my foot down.

(Greg comes back in.)

GREG: Hey, Sylvia, baby!

SYLVIA: *(Going to him, kissing him.)* I love you! I love you!

KATE: Did you make it up with Harold?

GREG: We agreed to disagree.

KATE: Oh Greg.

GREG: He keeps wanting to shift me into the money market.

KATE: What's wrong with that?

GREG: I'll tell you what's wrong with that. It's too abstract, that's what's wrong with that.

KATE: I don't see why.

GREG: Look, Kate. I liked manufacturing—starting off in product development. I liked that. I could see what we were making, I could touch it, I could tinker. And I liked selling, too, when they bumped me up to sales. I still knew the product. I could picture it in my mind. O.K. So then they acquire an investment company and tell me to trade. I try. I study up. I learn about oil, soybeans, corn. I read the forecasts, I figure the trends. I trade. And I do O.K. Not great, but I get by. But now they want me trade currencies, Kate. Money markets. Derivatives. I can't do that, sweetheart. What's behind currencies? Other currencies. What's behind them? Who knows? Nothing to touch, to see, to get a purchase on. And that's what I mean when I say it's too abstract.

KATE: Don't lose your job, Greg.

GREG: It wouldn't kill me.

KATE: The kids would have to quit school!

GREG: That wouldn't kill *them*.

KATE: Oh Greg.

GREG: I'm not so sure college is the answer to everything in life.

KATE: *You* went to college.

GREG: That's why I'm not so sure.

KATE: Oh for God's sake…

GREG: If they really want college, they'll find ways of paying for it. They might get more out of it, too.

KATE: I can't believe I'm hearing this!

GREG: Neither can I. That's what makes it so exciting. *(He waves furtively to Sylvia.)*

KATE: So how did you leave it with Harold, Greg?

GREG: I told him to put me in something real.

KATE: Real? What's real?

GREG: Sylvia's real, aren't you, Sylvia?

SYLVIA: *(Leaping into his arms.)* I sure try to be!

KATE: Down, Sylvia!…Make her get down, Greg!

GREG: *(Gently letting Sylvia down.)* Down, Sylvia.

KATE: She'll ruin your clothes.

GREG: Don't jump up, Sylvia.

SYLVIA: Sorry. I went a little overboard there.

GREG: Let me at least try her, Kate.

KATE: For how long?

GREG: A few days, at least.

KATE: All right. For a few days.

SYLVIA: Yippee! Yay! I sense a change in the weather here.

KATE: For a few days we will *try* Sylvia. In the fervent hope that you'll realize how dumb it is to take on a dog at this point in our lives.

GREG: Fair enough, Kate.

SYLVIA: *(Standing by Greg.)* You're happy, I'm happy.

KATE: No, now wait. I also want one thing clear, Greg: She's yours, not mine. I won't feed her, and I won't walk her, and I don't want her jumping onto any of the— *(Sees something on the floor.)* What's that?

GREG: What's what?

KATE: That puddle. She's pee'd, Greg.

GREG: Did you do that, Sylvia?

SYLVIA: I won't dignify that with an answer.

KATE: Of course she did that.

SYLVIA: I'm not saying a word.

GREG: She was nervous, Kate. Strange place. Hostile atmosphere…

SYLVIA: That's it. That was the problem.

KATE: You should punish her, Greg!

GREG: I can't punish her, it's too late to punish her.

SYLVIA: *(Hugging him.)* I love this man. I adore him.

KATE: Rub her nose in it at least! She's got to learn!

GREG: I won't do that, Kate!

SYLVIA: Hey! Hey! Hey!

KATE: Quiet, you!

SYLVIA: I'm getting nervous. I might bite.

GREG: No, now relax, Sylvia.

KATE: At least clean it up, Greg.

GREG: Glad to. *(He uses his newspaper.)*

SYLVIA: *(Watching him.)* This is slightly embarrassing.

KATE: Honestly! Springing a dog on me this way!

GREG: There! All cleaned up! See? Not a trace!

SYLVIA: Wasn't there, didn't happen.

KATE: You've really thrown me a curve here, Greg.

GREG: Tell you what: We'll go out.

KATE: Out? Now?

SYLVIA: Did I hear the word "out"?

GREG: *(To Kate.)* I meant Sylvia.

KATE: Oh.

GREG: *(To Sylvia.)* Let's go out, Sylvia.

SYLVIA: *(Leaping into his arms again.)* Knew it! Can't wait! Love going out!

GREG: Down, Sylvia! Down!

SYLVIA: *(Getting down.)* But it's my favorite thing!

KATE: *(Exiting to get cleaning equipment.)* What about the Waldmans?

SYLVIA: *(Finding her leash, handing it to him.)* Let's go, Greg.

GREG: *(Calling toward off.)* The Waldmans?

KATE: *(From within.)* Dinner! The concert!

SYLVIA: *(Dragging him toward the front hall.)* Come on, Greg!

GREG: *(Calling to Kate.)* Take Betsy in my place. She loves concerts.

KATE: *(Returning with a spray cleaner and a cloth.)* Sweetheart—

GREG: *(As he is pulled by Sylvia.)* Sylvia needs to go!

KATE: I'm worried, Greg. I'm worried about your job, I'm worried about you, I'm worried about us.

GREG: *(As he is dragged off by Sylvia.)* I'm worried about Sylvia at the moment.

KATE: *(Standing watching them.)* "I must be cruel, only to be kind. *(She kneels to clean up the spot.)* Thus bad begins… *(She sprays the "spot.")* …and worse remains behind." *Hamlet,* Act Three.

(Music: Nature music, such as Wagner's Siegfried Idyll. *Kate goes off as the set changes. Greenery. Bird sounds. Occasional sounds of dogs barking offstage. Greg and Sylvia come on, each holding an end of the leash.)*

GREG: Here we are, Sylvia. The park. Where we met. Remember?

SYLVIA: I'm nervous.

GREG: No. Hey, you're in your element now. This is nature, Sylvia. This is your natural habitat.

SYLVIA: I'm still nervous.

GREG: Look at those other dogs.

SYLVIA: I see them, I see them.

GREG: This is called Dog Hill. They allow dogs to play freely here. *(He takes the leash from her.)* Go play, Sylvia. *(Giving her a shove.)*

SYLVIA: Hey! Stop pushing.

GREG: Then go, Sylvia. There's your group, there's your pack. Call of the wild, kid.

SYLVIA: I know all that.

GREG: And you need the exercise.

SYLVIA: Look, it's no easy thing wading into a new group. They can gang up. Or bite. Or simply ignore you. I notice you're not barging into that group of dog owners.

GREG: You have a point.

SYLVIA: So. Let me take my own sweet time. *(She starts tentatively offstage.)*

GREG: *(Watching her go.)* Good girl. *(Continuing to watch.)* Good…Go on… Play…Run around…Good.

(Sylvia goes off. Tom comes on. He wears jeans, a windbreaker, and a base-ball cap.)

TOM: Hiya.

GREG: Hello.

TOM: New around here?

GREG: Just got a dog.

TOM: That one yours?

GREG: Right.

TOM: Cute.

GREG: Thanks.

TOM: Cute little butt on her.

GREG: I agree.

TOM: That's my Golden sniffing around her.

GREG: Good-looking dog.

TOM: His name's Bowser.

GREG: He looks like a Bowser.

TOM: He is. He is definitely a Bowser.

GREG: Mine's called Sylvia.

TOM: Sylvia?…Uh oh.

GREG: You don't like the name Sylvia?

TOM: Might cause problems.

GREG: Why?

TOM: Give a dog a woman's name, you begin to think of her as a woman.

GREG: Oh yes?

TOM: That can be dangerous. Which is why I go for doggy names. Spot. Fido. Bowser…Sylvia? That can spell trouble.

GREG: Oh come on.

TOM: Maybe I'm just associating. I had a girl named Sylvia.

GREG: Was she good-looking?

TOM: No, she was a dog.

(Both laugh; then both watch.)

GREG: They seem to be getting along.

TOM: Sylvia and Bowser. (Calling out.) Easy, Bowser. Go slow. (To Greg.) Is Sylvia spayed?

GREG: She's a stray. I haven't had her checked yet.

TOM: Don't let them spay her till you're sure she's been in heat.

GREG: Don't?

TOM: It's a feminist thing. You're supposed to let her experience how it feels to be female. That way, she'll retain a sense of gender later on.

GREG: Ah.

TOM: There's a book on the subject. Called *Play Now, Spay Later.* I'll bring it the next time I come to the park.

GREG: Thanks.

(Sylvia runs back on enthusiastically.)

SYLVIA: Just touching base here, just touching base.

GREG: Having a good time, Sylvia?

SYLVIA: The best!

GREG: Do you like Bowser?

SYLVIA: I think he's absolutely fantastic!

GREG: Then go back and play!

SYLVIA: May I?

GREG: Sure, kid! Go on! Shoo!

SYLVIA: Oh boy! Look out, Bowser! Here I come! *(She runs off.)*

TOM: She's a little insecure, isn't she?

GREG: Why do you say that?

TOM: The way she checks back with you.

GREG: She loves me.

TOM: Ah.

GREG: She thinks I saved her life. I'm her knight in shining armor.

TOM: Uh-oh.

GREG: Now what's the matter?

TOM: You married?

GREG: Sure. Why?

TOM: Wife fond of Sylvia?

GREG: Not yet. Why?

TOM: Kids out of the nest?

GREG: Right. Why?

TOM: Be careful.

GREG: What do you mean?

TOM: You can get lost in it.

GREG: Oh yes?

TOM: Sure. A man and his dog. It's a big thing.

GREG: I guess it is.

TOM: Women sense it. They nose it out. My wife feels very threatened by it.

GREG: She does?

TOM: Oh God yes. And I imagine it's worse with yours.

GREG: Why?

TOM: No offense, but you're older. With older guys, it can become major.

GREG: Think so?

TOM: Oh sure. It's something to hold onto, on the way down.

GREG: Oh now.

TOM: Look, women with dogs, no problem. A dog is basically another kid to them. It's a maternal thing. But for guys, it's different. When I come home at night, I have to *remind* myself to kiss my wife before I say hello to Bowser.

GREG: Mmm hmm.

TOM: I even think about him at work. I keep wanting to call him up and chew the fat. I don't think it's a gay thing, but I love that guy.

GREG: I can understand that.

TOM: And they say it's even worse if your dog's a female.

GREG: Really?

TOM: There was a guy here, had a dog named Debbie—half basset, half beagle—sweet little thing. His wife walked in on him giving Debbie a bath, and got so jealous she gave the dog away.

GREG: Christ! What did the guy do?

TOM: Sued her for damages. The judge was a dog owner and came down on his side. He said a man and his dog is a sacred relationship. What nature hath put together let no woman put asunder.

GREG: So what happened?

TOM: Well, the guy got Debbie back, and his wife back, and they all tried moving to Vermont. But it's still not good. Someone visited them recently and said it reminded him of the last chapter of *Ethan Frome*.

GREG: Good Lord.

TOM: There's a book out on the problem, actually. *Your Pooch and Your Partner.* It has one basic bit of advice. Always remember that your dog is simply a dog. Always keep reminding yourself of that fact. Not a person. Just a dog. Force yourself to think it. Otherwise you can get into deep dog shit.

GREG: Gotcha.

TOM: Well. Time to go. Better hold Sylvia so she won't follow Bowser.

GREG: Oh she won't do that.

TOM: She might. Bowser brings out the beast in them.

(He goes off. Music: something cozy and domestic, like "My Blue Heaven." Greg strolls off as the set becomes the apartment and Kate enters, settling at her desk.)

GREG: *(Calling from off.)* We're home!

KATE: Love that "we."

GREG: *(Coming on; he wears a different, more informal shirt.)* Well we are.

KATE: You're late again.

GREG: I lost track of the time.

KATE: This is the third time this week.

GREG: *(Kissing her.)* Time is for slaves, Katie.

KATE: Time is for people who have things to do. I have an evening meeting.

GREG: In the middle of August?

KATE: They're deciding to try a pilot program for my new English curriculum.

GREG: *(Kissing her.)* What? Hey! Congratulations! You're turning into a big cheese!

KATE: I try.

GREG: You do more than try! You succeed, baby!

KATE: Let's hope. *(She gathers up her books and papers.)* Anyway, I had to eat early. The microwave stands waiting.

GREG: Fine.

KATE: Where's Saliva?

GREG: Her name is Sylvia, Kate.

KATE: Where is she?

GREG: She's a little hyper at the moment. I put her in the other room.

KATE: No wonder things seemed so peaceful.

GREG: Katie. Before you go, I've got a surprise for you.

KATE: A surprise?

GREG: *(Taking her to the chair, sitting her down.)* Remember I said Sylvia was a little hyper?

KATE: I vaguely recall that observation, yes.

GREG: I'll show you why. *(He goes off.)*

KATE: *(Checking her watch; calling off.)* I haven't got much time, Greg. *(Greg comes back on.)*

GREG: Ta da. *(Calling off.)* Sylvia: Come. *(Proudly.)* I had her professionally groomed.

(Lush advertising music. Pink light. Sylvia comes on with a new hairdo, a bow in her hair, and a corny outfit.)

SYLVIA: Look at me! Look at me! *(Shimmying.)* How do you like them apples?

GREG: See why I was late? They gave her the full treatment: flea dip, nails clipped, ears cleaned, the works.

KATE: *(Dryly.)* Really?

GREG: They even evacuated her anal glands.

KATE: Spare me, Greg.

GREG: O.K. But the girl who gave her the bath said she thought she was basically French poodle.

(Sylvia leans against the arm of the couch and begins to sing a French cabaret song.)

GREG: They told me she was crawling with fleas. You were right about that, Katie. But now look at her. Isn't she spectacular?

(Sylvia starts another French song and jumps onto the couch.)

GREG: Don't you want to keep her now?

KATE: Off, Sylvia!

(Sylvia burrows her nose into the couch.)

GREG: Oh come on.

KATE: Off that couch, Sylvia! I don't want her on the furniture, Greg…OFF, Sylvia!

GREG: *(Bringing Sylvia to Kate.)* Smell her, Kate.

KATE: I don't want to smell her, Greg.

GREG: No really. She smells great. Come on. Smell.

KATE: I can smell her from here, sweetie.

GREG: Then don't you think she smells great?

KATE: She smells like a lavatory in an airplane, Greg.

GREG: Oh Kate.

KATE: All right. A lavatory in First Class.

GREG: At least you admit she's a class act.

SYLVIA: *(Holding out her hand to be kissed.)* Enchanté, Madame.

KATE: *(Rejecting the hand.)* I've really got to go.

GREG: *(Holding Sylvia up by her arms.)* But just *look* at her. Isn't she fucking gorgeous?

KATE: Greg, *don't* use that word, please, if you can possibly help it! I am spending my days trying to teach urban children the liberating possibilities of William Shakespeare in all his majesty and variety! I'd prefer not to come home to four letter words! *(She goes out.)*

SYLVIA: *(Looking after her.)* Dig *her.*

GREG: She's tired. She works hard.

SYLVIA: She doesn't like me.

GREG: She will, Sylvia.

SYLVIA: She makes me nervous. I sense the clock ticking away.

GREG: She just takes her time about things. Hey, it took her two years to say she'd marry me.

SYLVIA: Two *years?* Jesus, Greg! If you multiply that by seven why that's… um…carry the two…I make that fourteen years, dog time! That's too long, Greg!

GREG: She's worth it, Sylvia. I promise.

SYLVIA: Yeah, but can't I do something to speed things up, Greg? I'm tired of being just a house guest around here. I want to feel totally at home. *(She puts a tentative foot on the couch.)*

GREG: She'll come around. She's just a little career-oriented at the moment. It's a phase women are going through these days…Come on. Let's see what there is for chow.

(They go off, as we hear a telephone ringing. It is night. Kate comes on, wearing a bathrobe and carrying a portable phone.)

KATE: Hello?…Oh hello, Harold. No, it's never too late, Harold…No, he's fine. Why did you think he was sick?…What? The whole afternoon?…I didn't know that, Harold, no…Yes, well he's not here, Harold…He's out with the d-d-d—with a client, actually, Harold. Which, come to think of it, was where he was this afternoon…Is it that late? Well that must be because this client is a real party-animal…Yes, I'll tell Greg to stop by your office first thing…Good night, Harold. *(She hangs up; to herself.)* "Lord, Lord, how this world is given to lying." *Henry the Fourth, Part One.*

(She goes off as we hear urban and moody music. Urban setting, late at night. Greg and Sylvia come on, holding either end of the leash.)

GREG: Know something? I'm beginning to like these late night walks, Sylvia…They're turning into a whole new thing.

SYLVIA: Excuse me? I was concentrating on that Doberman across the street.

GREG: I was just saying that these walks at night are giving me a whole new perspective on life. The city seems to be shaking itself down to its essentials. That truck delivering tomorrow's vegetables. That doorman keeping watch over his flock by night. That young couple, hurrying home to screw. Food, shelter, sex. The basic things stand out at night, Sylvia.

SYLVIA: Now wait. Go slow here. I'm not quite with you, Greg.

GREG: Remember when we passed that poor homeless woman huddled in the doorway? Or that scruffy guy poking in the garbage for soft-drink cans? Remember how I made eye contact with them, Sylvia? We recognized each other in ways we could never do during the day.

SYLVIA: Want to run that by me one more time?

GREG: I just mean that when I'm out here at night with you, all the bustle of the daytime world seems like an old game of Trivial Pursuit.

(By now Sylvia's leash is tangled around her feet.)

GREG: I feel connected to my fellow creatures in a new and special way, Sylvia. *(He untangles her.)* I feel part of some larger pack. Surely you can understand that.

SYLVIA: Nope. Thought I had it, but it slipped away.

GREG: Maybe it's just the anxieties of middle age. Or the sense of disillusionment which goes with late twentieth-century capitalism. I mean, the Cold War's over, Sylvia. We've won. But what have we got?

SYLVIA: I wish I could contribute something here, but I just plain can't. *(She sits.)*

GREG: Never mind. Look, Sylvia! Look up there! Through all this urban haze, you can still see a star! How long has it been since we've really looked at the stars? Our early ancestors knew them cold, Sylvia. They could read them like books.

(Sylvia yawns.)

GREG: They used them to guide their way through forests, and across deserts, and over the vast expanses of the sea. Birds and animals know them too, I hear. Migrating geese, salmon, wildebeest...

SYLVIA: Huh?

GREG: I guess what I'm talking about is instinct, Sylvia. Maybe we have instincts we don't even know about. Maybe we are experiencing basic pulls we don't even recognize. Maybe that vast book of nature spread open above us is trying to tell us things we once knew, and have forgotten, and need to know again.

SYLVIA: Wow, Greg. Boy. Hmmm.

GREG: All I know is you trigger those instincts in me, Sylvia. You take me back in some basic way. Oh and hey, look! There's the moon! Catch that moon, Sylvia, rising between those buildings! How many people these days really notice the moon?

SYLVIA: I suppose you'd like me to sit down and howl at it.

GREG: I wouldn't mind.

SYLVIA: Well I don't think I can do that, Greg. Sorry. I like to think I've grown beyond that kind of behavior. *(She sniffs something.)* Excuse me, but I have to check my messages.

GREG: I'm thinking about quitting my job, Sylvia.

SYLVIA: Oh?

GREG: Chucking the whole thing.

SYLVIA: What would you do instead?

GREG: Something with you, maybe.

SYLVIA: I wouldn't mind going into advertising. How would you feel about being in one of those Ralph Lauren ads in the New York *Times Sunday Magazine?* You nursing a glass of scotch, me curled comfortably on some couch. I could do that, Greg.

GREG: No, Sylvia. No advertising, please. That's even worse than trading currencies.

We should do something more essential, Sylvia. Drug detection, maybe. Can you detect drugs?

SYLVIA: I'd sure like to try.

GREG: Or how about working with the blind. Or I could take you into nursing homes. Or children's wards in hospitals. Old people and kids, Sylvia. They're keyed into the essentials. They'd connect with you immediately.

SYLVIA: Hold it! *(She stops.)*

GREG: What?

SYLVIA: *(Looking out.)* There's something there.

GREG: Where?

SYLVIA: *(Bending over.)* There! There! Under that parked car.

GREG: I don't see...

SYLVIA: Hey, hey, hey!

GREG: *(Sees.)* Oh that. That's just a cat.

SYLVIA: Knew it!

GREG: Just an old pussycat.

SYLVIA: Let me at it.

GREG: *(Holding her leash.)* Easy now.

SYLVIA: I said let me at that thing. I want to kill that fucker.

GREG: *(Holding her back.)* No, Sylvia. No.

SYLVIA: *(To the cat.)* Hey you! Hey kitty! You're a sack of shit, you know that?

GREG: Let's move on, Sylvia.

SYLVIA: You're disgusting, kitty! You're a disgrace to the animal kingdom!

GREG: Leave it, Sylvia. Let's move along!

SYLVIA: *(Backing away.)* Smell that damn thing! Can you smell it? I can smell it from here! *(Coming down again.)* You stink, kitty! Take a bath sometime!

GREG: Now, now.

SYLVIA: *(Now looking at the cat upside down.)* Who are you staring at, you sneaky bastard? You staring at me?

GREG: *(Dragging her away.)* Let's go, Sylvia!

SYLVIA: *(Over her shoulder to the cat.)* Fuck you, kitty! Up yours with a ten-foot pole!

GREG: Come on now.

SYLVIA: *(To the cat.)* You should be chased up a tree, you cocksucker! I'd like to bite off your tail and shove it up your ass! I hate your fucking guts, kitty, and don't you ever forget it! *(Turning to Greg. Suddenly very sweetly.)* Well. Out of sight, out of mind. Let's move on.

GREG: Wow, Sylvia.

SYLVIA: I'm sorry, but I had to do it.

GREG: You're full of surprises, aren't you?

SYLVIA: You want instinct, you got instinct.

GREG: I sure did.

SYLVIA: A whiff of the jungle, right? Nature, tooth and claw.

GREG: I'll say.

SYLVIA: I must say it helps to express your feelings.

GREG: I should say that stuff to Harold at work. How does it go again? You're a sack of shit, Harold! You're a disgrace to the—

SYLVIA: *(Interrupting.)* Hey look! Here comes that corgi from over on Columbus Avenue. Shall I sidle up to him or ignore him completely?

GREG: Surprise me, Sylvia. Surprise me.

(They go off. Night. An airport waiting area. Airport music. Sounds of a jet taking off Kate comes on in a raincoat, carrying her bag, paces, checks her watch. Blurry announcement on loudspeaker: "American Airlines Flight 203 to Indianapolis has been temporarily delayed." After a moment, Greg joins Kate.)

GREG: They said there'd be a short delay.

KATE: Damn. *(Sitting down; taking out her work.)* Well, that gives me more time to prepare for the conference. You should go home, sweetie. *(She starts to work.)*

GREG: I'll stick around. In case you're canceled.

KATE: You don't have to.

GREG: *(Sitting beside her.)* I want to.

KATE: You shouldn't even have bothered to drive me out.

GREG: I wanted to.

KATE: You wanted an excuse to skip that dinner with those clients.

GREG: I wanted to be with you.

KATE: I really should do some work.

GREG: Go ahead. I'll just sit with you.

(Kate works for a moment.)

KATE: What about her holiness?

GREG: Who? Oh. Sylvia. What about her?

KATE: I thought she hated to be left alone.

GREG: I can't be with her every minute.

KATE: That's good to know.

GREG: She'll get me all to herself while you're gone.

KATE: Goodie-goodie.

GREG: Besides, she has to learn to be alone occasionally. You'd think I was going to the moon the way she looked when I left tonight. I kept saying I'd just be gone a little while, but she gave me this soulful look which—

KATE: All right, all right. I'm sorry I brought it up.

(She works on her report. Greg stares off into space. The airport music modulates into a piano accompaniment. Sylvia appears, settled comfortably on the couch.)

SYLVIA: *(On the couch; singing.)*

"Ev'ry time we say good-bye I die a little,

Ev'ry time we say good-bye I wonder why a little,

Why the gods above me

Who must be in the know

Think so little of me

They'd allow you to go…"

GREG: *(Singing, as Kate works beside him.)*

"When you're near there's such an air of spring about it

I can hear a lark somewhere begin to sing about it,

There's no love song finer,

But how strange the change from major to minor

Ev'ry time we say good-bye."

(Loudspeaker announcement: "Flight 231 to Indianapolis is now boarding." The music continues underneath.)

KATE: *(Putting her work away.)* Wooops. There's my plane. Guess I'm off. *(Gets up; kisses him.)* Good-bye, darling. See you Wednesday night.

GREG: *(Getting up; kissing her.)* I'll miss you.

KATE: Oh sure.

GREG: Really. I will.

(Kate moves off, as if to get into line to board. Greg looks after her. Music comes up.)

KATE: *(Singing; holding her ticket.)*

"Ev'ry time we say good-bye I die a little,

Ev'ry time we say good-bye I wonder why a little,"

GREG: *(Singing toward Kate.)*

"Why the gods above me who must be in the know,

Think so little of me they'd allow you to go…"

GREG AND KATE: *(Together.)*

"When you're near there's such an air of spring about it…"

SYLVIA: *(Still on the couch.)*

"I can hear a lark somewhere begin to sing about it,"

ALL THREE:

> "There's no love song finer,
> But how strange the change from major to minor
> Ev'ry time we say good-bye."

(Kate goes off one way, Greg the other. Sylvia remains on the couch.)

SYLVIA: *(Suddenly alert.)* Hey, hey hey! *(Ultimate relief.)* Knew it! It's him! He's home!

(She runs off eagerly as the music ends. Music: Urban and hectic. Daytime. The apartment. Phyllis comes in. She wears a light-colored jacket.)

PHYLLIS: *(Looking around.)* This is lovely, Kate. I was expecting something more naive. I mean, for new arrivals. I mean, sometimes when people come to New York, they bring the provinces with them. I have a friend who moved from Tampa and brought her entire collection of sea shells. There were shells on the tables, shells on the chairs, shells everywhere you looked. I said, these shells are lovely, Sheila, but where do you shit?—I mean, sit. I mean...

(Kate comes on, carrying a stack of mail.)

PHYLLIS: I like your apartment, Kate.

KATE: *(Laughing.)* Well it's simple and convenient. *(She crosses to her desk.)* Anybody here?...No, thank God. They must be in the park. For the umpteenth time.

PHYLLIS: Who?

KATE: Don't get me started...But how lucky we ran into each other on the street, Phyllis!

PHYLLIS: *(Starting to take off her jacket.)* That's New York for you. The biggest small town in the world.

KATE: I'm discovering that.

PHYLLIS: Well now you and Greg are here, Hamilton and I want to give you a small dinner party. *(Phyllis is about to toss her jacket onto the couch.)*

KATE: WAIT!

PHYLLIS: What?

KATE: Not there! *(Takes the jacket.)* You'll ruin that nice jacket. She leaves these great, grubby hairs. *(She carries the jacket off.)*

PHYLLIS: Who?

KATE: *(From off.)* Sylvia.

PHYLLIS: Sylvia?

KATE: *(Returning.)* The dog.

PHYLLIS: Oh. *(She checks where to sit.)* You let the dog onto the couch?

KATE: *(Brushing off the couch.)* I do not. I absolutely forbid it. But she...I'd prefer not to talk about it.

PHYLLIS: Good for you. We New Yorkers all have parts of our lives we keep to ourselves. I mean, we all have private parts. I mean...

KATE: *(Laughing.)* You haven't changed since Vassar, Phyllis...I hear you and Hamilton are the toast of the East Side.

PHYLLIS: Oh well. We circulate...Who would you like to meet? Kitty Carlisle Hart? Charlayne Hunter Gault? Boutros Boutros-Ghali?

KATE: Anyone interested in the New York schools.

PHYLLIS: Fine. I'll organize an evening which will focus strictly on the educational—

KATE: She waits, you know. She literally waits, until I'm out the door, and then she leaps onto that couch.

PHYLLIS: The dog?

KATE: Sylvia. And when she hears my key in the latch, she jumps off.

PHYLLIS: Are you sure?

KATE: I am. Once I sneaked back in, and caught her red-handed.

PHYLLIS: I hope you punished her immediately.

KATE: I tried. But she practically laughed in my face. She only listens to Greg.

PHYLLIS: Then Greg should punish her. Dogs are like children. They need to be thoroughly disciplined from the ground up.

KATE: Greg? Discipline Sylvia? Don't make me laugh.

PHYLLIS: *(Takes her memo book out of her purse.)* Let's talk dates for the party. Hamilton and I are booked solid... *(Flips through pages.)* ...through October, but how about November 6th?

KATE: Fine.

PHYLLIS: *(Writing it in.)* Good. There are no friends like old—

KATE: I have the strong suspicion that when I'm out of the apartment, they sit on the couch *together.*

PHYLLIS: Greg and Sylvia?

KATE: They do everything together. Once I caught them sharing an ice cream cone.

PHYLLIS: How disgusting!

KATE: And she uses his hairbrush. I mean, he uses it. On her.

PHYLLIS: Hamilton has taken up goldfish.

KATE: At least they stay in their bowl.

PHYLLIS: Not necessarily.

KATE: What?

PHYLLIS: Sometimes he takes them into the bathtub.

KATE: No!

PHYLLIS: I swear! If you bring it up, he'll deny it, but I swear I caught him at it.

KATE: Good Lord.

PHYLLIS: Look at us! Here we are talking about animals when we should be planning our party.

KATE: You're absolutely right. Let's have a drink. What would you like, Phyllis? Wine? Vodka? What?

PHYLLIS: Just fizzy water, please. I'm trying to give up alcohol.

KATE: Good for you. I'll get it. *(She goes off.)*

PHYLLIS: *(Toward off.)* Now fill me in on this school thing, Kate. I saw Madge MacKenzie at the Colony Club and she says you're roaming around Harlem, reciting Shakespeare.

(Kate returns with two glasses.)

KATE: That's why I want to meet people with pull, Phyllis. I'm trying to put Shakespeare into the junior high curriculum.

PHYLLIS: Is that possible? I mean, at that age? I mean, these days? I mean, up there?

KATE: I hope so. If we can hook children in junior high, we might have them for life, Phyllis.

PHYLLIS: I wish I could believe that, Kate.

KATE: It's not just Shakespeare, Phyllis. It's language in general. These kids are fascinated by words. They rap, they rhyme, they invent these exciting phrases and metaphors just the way Shakespeare did. If we can take their energy and curiosity and imagination, and give them words, more words, good words in significant contexts, then maybe— *(Pause.)* She wants to sleep in our bed, you know.

PHYLLIS: Sylvia?

KATE: Sylvia wants to sleep in our bed.

PHYLLIS: You said no, I hope.

KATE: Of course I said no. Not even outside the covers.

PHYLLIS: I should hope not.

KATE: But Greg fought me all the way. And continues to, on every issue. When we visited our friends the Wardwells up in Williamstown, he insisted on taking her with us.

PHYLLIS: At least it's the country.

KATE: But it was our *anniversary*, Phyllis! How would you like to be driving through that lovely New England scenery with Sylvia drooling down the back of your neck.

PHYLLIS: I see your point.

KATE: And when we arrived, the Wardwells put us all in the same room.

PHYLLIS: You and Greg and Sylvia?

KATE: There we were, holed up together. Greg and I spent our wedding anniversary with Sylvia wandering restlessly around the room, peering over the bed, and panting.

PHYLLIS: How horrible.

KATE: I mean, here I am, breaking my back trying to instill some sense of civility in American life and…She drinks from the john, you know.

PHYLLIS: Sylvia.

KATE: She drinks from the toilet. Sometimes, when we're trying to have a decent dinner, you can hear these great gulping sounds coming from the loo.

PHYLLIS: Good heavens.

KATE: Then she comes back in, and sits slobbering by the table, eyeing us all through the meal.

PHYLLIS: You see? They're like children. They have to be exiled while we eat.

KATE: Don't I wish. *(Getting up.)* But how about a refill, Phyllis?

PHYLLIS: I'm fine, thanks.

KATE: I might just shift to a little Scotch. Excuse me a minute. *(She goes off.)*

PHYLLIS: *(Toward off.)* Now be careful, Kate. Don't start leaning on liquor. Take it from one who knows. It's the curse of our generation and it's the curse of our particular ethnic group.

KATE: *(Coming back in with a glass of Scotch.)* He takes Sylvia out to lunch, you know.

PHYLLIS: No.

KATE: He dashes home at noon and they go out to lunch. He's found some restaurant on Amsterdam Avenue which is willing to serve Sylvia.

PHYLLIS: I'm appalled!

KATE: And lately he's been taking the afternoon off.

PHYLLIS: Hamilton sometimes does that. He sneaks down to the aquarium.

KATE: But Greg does this every day! He and Sylvia have lunch, and then they go on these long walks. He covers the entire city. He says that with Sylvia he meets all sorts of people, from all walks of life. He says he's having a truly democratic experience for the first time in his life.

PHYLLIS: I thought Greg was a Republican.

KATE: He was! He used to be.

PHYLLIS: Hamilton at least is that.

KATE: I almost wish Greg would change back.

PHYLLIS: I think all men should be Republicans, Kate. It seems to be good for their prostate. When Hamilton voted for Bush, why he—I can't wait for the next erection—I mean, election…Ah, but I've been talking too much.

KATE: I think I hate Sylvia, Phyllis.

PHYLLIS: No.

KATE: I do. I never thought I could hate anybody except Nixon. But now I hate Sylvia.

PHYLLIS: She's just a dog, Kate.

KATE: I don't care if she's a kangaroo. She's destroying our marriage.

PHYLLIS: Oh now.

KATE: Sometimes I want to kill her, Phyllis. I want to put De-Con in her dog dish.

PHYLLIS: Now that's a little drastic.

KATE: But I feel doomed, Phyllis. Cooped up in this small apartment with that creature.

PHYLLIS: Then draw the line, Kate. Say she's simply got to go.

KATE: I've tried. We keep making these clear agreements. But Greg keeps breaking them. Like Hitler.

PHYLLIS: Oh Kate.

KATE: I have the terrible feeling I'll be sharing my life with her for another ten years.

PHYLLIS: Do you think she'll last that long?

KATE: I know she will. But I won't. If this continues, she'll stand drooling over my grave.

(Greg's voice is heard off.)

GREG: *(From off.)* Hello!

KATE: There they are. *(Calls off.)* Phyllis Cutler is here, dear! *(To Phyllis.)* Now brace yourself.

(Greg comes in.)

GREG: Here we are…Why, Phyllis! Hello! Good to see you again!

(They shakes hands. Sylvia rushes in.)

GREG: This is Sylvia.

SYLVIA: Hello, hello, hello. *(She runs to Phyllis and immediately starts kneeing Phyllis's crotch.)* Nice crotch here. Nice crotch.

PHYLLIS: *(Trying to protect herself.)* Run along, Sylvia!

SYLVIA: *(Kneeing her.)* This is just my way of saying hello.

KATE: Stop it, Sylvia!

GREG: Down, Sylvia!

KATE: Greg, make her stop.

GREG: *(Pulling Sylvia away.)* DOWN, Sylvia! NO, NO.

KATE: *(To Phyllis.)* See what I mean?

PHYLLIS: I'm beginning to.

GREG: *(To Phyllis.)* She doesn't normally do that.

KATE: She does it all the time!

GREG: Hey listen! We've learned three new tricks today. Want to see them?

KATE: We do not.

GREG: Phyllis wants to see them, don't you, Phyllis?

PHYLLIS: Well I—

KATE: Wait. How did you have time to teach Sylvia tricks, Greg?

GREG: I came home early.

    (Kate and Phyllis glance at each other.)

KATE: Why, Greg?

GREG: So I could teach Sylvia tricks.

KATE: *(To Phyllis.)* See?

GREG: We found a quiet place in the park and practiced, didn't we, Sylvia?

SYLVIA: We did, we did.

GREG: So. First trick. Where's your little red ball, Sylvia?

SYLVIA: Huh?

GREG: *(Pulling the ball partly out of his pants pocket.)* Find your little red ball.

SYLVIA: Oh. Gotcha. *(She goes to his pocket and takes out the little red ball. She holds it up to the others.)* See? Little red ball.

GREG: Now give it to Daddy.

SYLVIA: *(Coyly.)* Why should I?

GREG: Give it to Daddy, Sylvia.

SYLVIA: What's in it for me?

GREG: Here's a treat if you give that ball back to Daddy, Sylvia.

SYLVIA: O.K. *(She gives him the ball.)*

GREG: Good girl. *(He gives her a treat.)*

SYLVIA: Thanks.

GREG: Now catch the ball, Sylvia.

SYLVIA: I'm still eating.

GREG: Catch the ball, Sylvia. *(He tosses the ball. Sylvia catches it.)* Good girl!

SYLVIA: *(To others.)* That was a tough one. *(She gives him back the ball.)*

GREG: *(Hugging her.)* You are a very good girl!

    (Tosses the ball offstage; Kate and Phyllis duck.)

GREG: Now. Go fetch, Sylvia.

SYLVIA: Go fetch that ball?

GREG: Go fetch that ball.

SYLVIA: All right, I will. Seeing as how you're God. *(She runs off.)*

KATE: *(To Phyllis.)* You see what I'm up against? Notice how all conversation stops. Notice how civilization completely collapses. While we wait for Sylvia.

PHYLLIS: I might just have a small Scotch, Kate.

KATE: Phyllis...

PHYLLIS: I want one, Kate. *(Grimly.)* Right now! *(Apologetically.)* Please. *(Kate looks at her and goes off.)*

GREG: *(To Phyllis.)* You're worried, aren't you?

PHYLLIS: Actually, I am, Greg.

GREG: Don't be. She'll find her ball. It's probably under the hall table. *(Sylvia comes back on with the ball.)*

GREG: See? What did I tell you.

PHYLLIS: I am ultimately relieved.

SYLVIA: Here's the ball, Greg.

GREG: *(Taking it.)* Thank you, Sylvia. Good girl. Now when Kate gets back, I want you to roll over.

SYLVIA: I don't like rolling over, Greg.

GREG: I know. But I want you to do it. *(Kate comes back with Phyllis's Scotch and the bottle.)*

KATE: Here you are, Phyllis.

PHYLLIS: *(Grabbing it.)* Thank you. *(She takes a big gulp.)*

KATE: Greg, I think we might put Sylvia—

GREG: Hold it. Watch this. Roll over, Sylvia.

SYLVIA: *(Confidingly.)* This is the one I don't like, Greg.

GREG: *(Taking a treat out of his pocket.)* Go on, Sylvia. Do it. Roll over. And you get a treat.

SYLVIA: All right. I'll do it. But I really hate this one. *(She gets down on the floor and does a reluctant and awkward rollover.)* I feel like a fool, but there you have it.

GREG: Good girl!

SYLVIA: Pay up, then.

GREG: Here you are, Sylvia. Here you are. *(To Kate and Phyllis.)* See? See what we accomplished?

SYLVIA: Did you like that trick, Phyllis? *(She goes for Phyllis's crotch again.)*

PHYLLIS: Go away, Sylvia!

KATE: Sylvia, stop that!

PHYLLIS: Have you tried spanking her? I don't think there's enough spanking these days. *(She takes another big gulp of her drink.)*

KATE: *(To Greg.)* Darling, do you think we possibly might put Sylvia in the kitchen. I mean, we want to talk to Phyllis, don't we?

GREG: Wait. Just one more trick.

(Kate pours another drink. Greg gets out another treat.)

GREG: Speak, Sylvia.

SYLVIA: Speak?

GREG: Speak, Sylvia.

SYLVIA: *(To Kate and Phyllis.)* I'm not sure what he wants here.

GREG: Speak, Sylvia. SPEAK.

SYLVIA: Now wait...I'm sure I know this one...I've just forgotten...

GREG: Look at this treat, Sylvia...You get it if you speak.

SYLVIA: It's coming back to me.

GREG: Speak, Sylvia.

SYLVIA: Hey!

GREG: Good girl.

SYLVIA: Hey! Hey!

GREG: Good girl!

SYLVIA: Hey! Hey! Hey!

GREG: *(Giving her the treat.)* That's a very good girl, Sylvia!

SYLVIA: *(Chewing.)* I knew I could do it.

GREG: *(To Kate.)* See, sweetie? She can speak!

KATE: *(To Phyllis.)* So much for Shakespeare.

PHYLLIS: *(Downing her drink.)* I've got to go. *(She gets up, stumbles, recovers.)*

KATE: But we've hardly talked.

PHYLLIS: I've got to be off. Really. *(Kisses her.)* So nice to see you again, Kate. *(Shakes hands with Greg.)* Good-bye, Greg. *(Waves at Sylvia.)* Bye, bye Sylvia. *(Sylvia goes for Phyllis's crotch once more.)*

KATE: No, Sylvia! NO!

GREG: Down, girl. *(To Phyllis.)* She likes you a lot, Phyllis.

PHYLLIS: I'll tell them that at my next A.A. meeting. *(Phyllis staggers out, quite smashed. Sylvia runs after her. We hear Phyllis's protests offstage. Kate goes off then returns angrily.)*

KATE: She is driving away our friends, Greg!

GREG: Oh come on.

KATE: She is, Greg. She gave Alice Felker a bloody nose.

GREG: She thought Alice was playing.

KATE: Well Alice wasn't. Alice was defending herself. *(Sylvia comes back on.)*

SYLVIA: I'd like to eat, please. Time to chow down.

KATE: Our friends loathe her.

GREG: The Wardwells loved her. They specifically said the next time we came up, be sure to bring Sylvia.

KATE: They were just being nice.

GREG: They loved her. Most people love her. People stop me in the street to pat her. Children's faces brighten as we walk by. She lightens my life.

KATE: She darkens mine, Greg.

SYLVIA: Where's dinner? I'm going to check on dinner. *(She goes out.)*

GREG: *(Starting to follow her.)* She's hungry.

KATE: *(Her Scotches are catching up with her.)* I want to talk about this, Greg.

GREG: We've been all through it.

KATE: We have *not* been all through it. *(She sits him down in the chair.)* Did you get fired today, Greg?

GREG: What?

KATE: Did you get fired?

GREG: What makes you think that?

KATE: I have an instinct. Did you get fired.

GREG: No! Of course not. No. *(Pause.)* I got temporarily laid off.

KATE: Oh Greg.

GREG: They gave me a leave of absence for medical reasons.

KATE: *Medical* reasons?

GREG: They think I need counseling.

KATE: *(Kneeling beside him.)* You do, darling! I really think you do!

GREG: Just because my work doesn't seem real any more.

KATE: What is real then, Greg?

GREG: Sylvia. Sylvia's real.

KATE: I'll tell you what's real, Greg. The mortgage on this apartment is real. The kids' tuitions are very, very real.

GREG: I need to feel more…

KATE: More what, Greg. And don't say "real."

GREG: More connected, then.

KATE: Connected…Connected to what?

GREG: Life. *(Pause.)* No. *(Pause.)* Living.

KATE: I'm beginning to understand, darling.

GREG: You are?

KATE: I am, sweetie. This is another one of those things that happen to men in middle age.

GREG: No it isn't.

KATE: Yes it is, darling. I admit I'm slightly sauced, but I still know a hawk from a handsaw.

GREG: What?

KATE: It's like when poor fat old Ted Donahue tried to take up tap dancing.

GREG: *(Getting up.)* This is entirely different.

KATE: *(Getting up; slurring her words.)* Well I'm sorry, sweetie, but whatever it is…I have to say time's up.

GREG: Time's up?

KATE: Really up. I said I'd try, and I have, and it's been much longer than a few days. So I'm putting my foot down, Greg. I want you to give Sylvia away.

GREG: Away?

KATE: I want that. I am asking that. I insist upon that.

GREG: What do you mean, give her *away?* To whom?

KATE: Some farmer. Give her to some farmer.

GREG: There are no farmers any more, Kate. Farmers don't exist. Read *The New Republic.*

KATE: Oh now…

GREG: And I refuse to give my dog to some agricultural conglomerate. Sylvia? Being cared for by Archer-Daniels-Midland? Nope. Sorry. Can't do it.

KATE: Greg…

(Sylvia comes in, carrying a woman's shoe.)

SYLVIA: Look what I've got!

KATE: Oh Lord, she's got my shoe.

GREG: It's a peace offering.

KATE: It is not! It's a deliberate act of aggression.

SYLVIA: *(Parading it around.)* Look at this shoe! Look at this fabulous shoe!

KATE: Drop that, Sylvia! Right now!

SYLVIA: Chase me.

KATE: She'll ruin it, Greg.

SYLVIA: Chase me.

GREG: She just wants to play.

KATE: *(Chasing her around the couch.)* I want that shoe, Sylvia. Immediately.

GREG: Bring it here, Sylvia.

(Sylvia finally brings the shoe to Greg; drops it at his feet.)

GREG: Good girl! *(Greg picks up the shoe, brings it to Kate.)* Here's your shoe, Katie.

KATE: *(Looking at the shoe.)* She's ruined it.

GREG: It's an old shoe.

KATE: *(On the verge of tears.)* It's my best pair! You owe me a new pair of shoes, Greg!

GREG: O.K. O.K. I'll buy you some shoes.

KATE: I'll bet she took my book, too.

GREG: What book?

KATE: My annotated copy of *All's Well That Ends Well.* I can't find it. I'll bet Sylvia took it and ate it.

GREG: She wouldn't do that.

SYLVIA: Hey! Hey! Hey!

KATE: She ate half *The New Yorker!*

GREG: It was a lousy issue anyway. *The New Yorker's* getting—

SYLVIA: Hey, hey!

KATE: Greg, I am issuing an ultimatum.

GREG: *(Starting out.)* It's time for her dinner. *(To Sylvia.)* Come on, sweetheart. Time to eat.
(They hurry off.)

KATE: *(Calling after.)* Sweetheart? Is it *sweetheart* now? Goddammit, Greg! When's the last time you said that to *me?*
(She throws the shoe after him, then sits down hopelessly, polishing off whatever glasses of liquor are available. After a moment, Sylvia comes back on, carrying the shoe.)

SYLVIA: I believe this is yours. *(She drops the shoe at Kate's feet.)*

KATE: Sylvia, I have something to say to you.

SYLVIA: What if I don't feel like listening?

KATE: Then I'll see to it that you never lick another plate.

SYLVIA: *(Getting onto the couch.)* All right. Shoot.

KATE: Off the couch, please.

SYLVIA: Greg lets me sit here.

KATE: I don't. Off! Right now!

SYLVIA: Make me.
(Kate moves toward her.)

SYLVIA: I'm warning you! I've been known to bite!

KATE: *(Almost falling over onto the couch.)* Try that just once, Sylvia! Just ONCE! And you are out the door! Now OFF! Right now!

SYLVIA: O.K. Cool it. I get the picture. *(She reluctantly gets off the couch.)* You sure don't like me, do you?

KATE: I think it's safe to say I hate your guts.

SYLVIA: May I ask why?

KATE: Because you're messing around with my marriage

(Sound of Greg offstage, banging a dish.)

GREG: *(From off.)* Din-din! Come and get it!

(Sylvia starts off.)

SYLVIA: I believe I'm wanted in the kitchen.

KATE: *(Making a lunge for Sylvia; they both fall to the floor.)* Hold it, Sylvia.

SYLVIA: Let me go!

KATE: I plan to do everything I can to get you out of here, Sylvia.

SYLVIA: I doubt if you can do very much, Kate.

(Both are now on their hands and knees.)

KATE: Before long you're going to be cowering in some cage.

GREG: *(From off.)* Dinny-poo! Sup-sup-suppertime!

SYLVIA: My master's voice, Kate.

KATE: *(Holding onto her.)* I'm not through yet, Sylvia. Now you should know that all you are is a male menopausal moment. Oh, I know, I know, it's all been very exciting, walking around town during these fine fall days. But when winter comes, Sylvia, when it's cold in the morning and dark in the afternoon, when he has to stand shivering in the park waiting to pick up your do-do, how long do you think you'll last, Sylvia? He'll have second thoughts then, Sylvia, and I'll be right there to help him think them.

(Sylvia struggles to get away.)

GREG: *(From off.)* Sylvia! Come! Kibble time!

SYLVIA: You're forgetting one thing, Kate.

KATE: Oh. And what is that, Sylvia?

SYLVIA: He loves me.

KATE: Oh yes?

SYLVIA: He does. He thinks I shit ice cream!

KATE: There's love and there's love, sister!

SYLVIA: Yes, well, we'll see.

KATE: Yes we'll see, Sylvia. From here on in, it's a fight to the finish.

SYLVIA: Fair enough! And may the best species win!

(They confront each other on all fours. Greg comes in, carrying a dog dish filled with kibble.)

GREG: *(Seeing them.)* Hey! Great! Can I play, too?

(He drops to his hands and knees, next to them. Kate looks at him. Quick black out.)

END OF ACT I

ACT II

Music: Something like "Autumn in New York." A suggestion of autumn foliage. Warm light. The Park. Bird sounds. Dogs yapping offstage. Greg sits on a park bench, basking in the autumn sun. Sylvia paces beside him.

GREG: Don't you want to play with the gang?

SYLVIA: I get bored with the afternoon crowd. Nannies and babies. Schnauzers and cocker spaniels.

GREG: What you mean is, Bowser hasn't shown up yet.

SYLVIA: I mean what I mean. *(She settles beside him on the bench.)*

GREG: I wish I knew more about you, Sylvia.

SYLVIA: Why do you have to know everything?

GREG: Just for the pleasure of knowing. Take Kate, for example. We started dating in high school. We know each other cold.

SYLVIA: Yeah well, that's her, this is me.

GREG: I wish I knew more about your former owner.

SYLVIA: Second owners always wish that.

GREG: Did you like him as much as you like me?

SYLVIA: How do you know it was a guy?

GREG: Good point. But you were mistreated, weren't you?

SYLVIA: I got to sleep on the couch.

GREG: Still. What kind of person would take you to the park and just let you go?

SYLVIA: How do you know I wasn't lost? Or how do you know I didn't see you sitting on a bench, and simply say to myself, "There's the man I want to spend the rest of my life with." How do you know I didn't break my leash and run to your side?

GREG: I don't know, do I?

SYLVIA: And you never will. See? I'm a mystery. I'm what's known as the Other. That's never happened to you before. That's why I'm so exciting. And that's what love is all about. Now go with the flow, man.

(Louder barking and yapping offstage. Sylvia gets up, and stretches.)

SYLVIA: Well. Now I think I'll just mosey on back to the group.

GREG: *(Looking off.)* Ah. Because Bowser's there now. Right?

SYLVIA: I'm not saying a word.

(She runs off. Greg stands and watches her. Tom comes on.)

TOM: Hiya, Greg.

GREG: Hi, Tom.

TOM: How're things going at home?

GREG: Fine.

TOM: Really?

GREG: Actually, not so good.

TOM: Thought so. Think I know why.

GREG: Sylvia's why.

TOM: *(Sitting beside him on the bench.)* No, no. It's deeper than that. I've been reading this book.

GREG: Another book.

TOM: This one's deep, man. It's all about us.

GREG: Us?

TOM: It says we're basically biophilic.

GREG: *(Moving away from him on the bench.)* Hey. Watch it.

TOM: No that's good, man. People who love dogs are biophiles. They're lovers of the *bios*—which is Greek for the processes of nature.

GREG: Go on.

TOM: What's more, the whole thing's genetic. Did your Dad take you fishing and hiking when you were young?

GREG: Actually yes.

TOM: Did your mother push your stroller through some zoo?

GREG: I'm sure. Yes.

TOM: See? What they were doing was activating your biophilic gene.

GREG: I see.

TOM: We've inherited these genes from our caveman days when we had to connect with nature in order to survive in it.

GREG: Ah.

TOM: And your relationship with Sylvia has reactivated that gene. That's why you respond to her so strongly. On the other hand, your wife's biophilic gene has become thoroughly atrophied.

GREG: That's true enough.

TOM: She sees nature as threatening and messy.

GREG: You got it.

TOM: That's why you're having marital problems. It's all built in. It's as if you were straight and she was gay. Or vice versa.

GREG: *(Uneasily.)* I don't know, Tom…

TOM: *(Getting up.)* Look. I'm just giving you a name for what's going on. Naming the problem helps you deal with it. Actually, that's why my wife and I have decided to split.

GREG: Oh, I'm sorry.

TOM: No, no, it's good. Biophiles need to mate with other biophiles. It's better for the environment. Bowser and I are hoping to hook up with a Forestry major.

GREG: Good luck.

TOM: I'll lend you the book.

GREG: *(Getting up; looking out.)* Sylvia's having a ball out there.

TOM: Life of the party, isn't she?

GREG: She's been to the beauty parlor again.

(Both watch.)

TOM: Or else she's in heat.

GREG: Naw.

TOM: She may be.

GREG: What makes you think so?

TOM: The way she carries her tush.

(They watch.)

TOM: Did you ever get her spayed?

GREG: Not yet. I took your advice about waiting.

(They watch.)

GREG: Is Bowser fixed?

TOM: Nope. It's different.

GREG: Is it?

(They watch.)

TOM: Call her. See if she'll come.

GREG: Of course she'll come.

TOM: Not if she's in heat.

GREG: *(Calling.)* Sylvia!…Sylvia, come! *(To Tom.)* See? She's coming immediately.

(Sylvia comes on.)

SYLVIA: Hi, Greg! *(To Tom.)* Hello, Tom. Did I ever tell you how fond I was of Bowser?

GREG: You're not in heat, are you, sweetheart?

SYLVIA: Me? Naw. No way.

GREG: Didn't think so.

SYLVIA: *(To herself.)* I just feel like fucking, that's all.

TOM: She seems to be asking for it.

GREG: She's just being affectionate.

SYLVIA: *(To herself.)* I want to fuckie-fuck-fuck.

TOM: I think she's definitely in heat.

GREG: It's just natural affection.

SYLVIA: May I go now?

GREG: Sure, Sylvia. Go play.

SYLVIA: *(Going off.)* Hey Bowser! Ready or not, here I come! And I want to fuck toot sweet! *(She runs off.)*

(Pause.)

GREG: You may be right. She may be in heat.

TOM: I think she is.

GREG: What do I do if she is?

TOM: Keep her inside.

GREG: With my *wife?*

TOM: Then send her away.

GREG: My wife?

TOM: Sylvia!

GREG: I'm not going to send her away.

TOM: Just for the duration.

GREG: Out of the question.

TOM: Then keep her on a leash at all times. And don't bring her into the park. If you let her loose, you're just asking for— *(Looks out.)* Uh oh.

GREG: What?

TOM: Where's Bowser?

GREG: Where's Sylvia?

(They look around.)

TOM: *(Finally.)* Look. Over there. Behind that bush.

(They look.)

GREG: Shit.

TOM: I told you!

GREG: *(Starting off.)* I'll break it up!

TOM: *(Holding him.)* Too late. They're locked.

GREG: I don't care. I've got to—

TOM: You'd hurt her.

GREG: But...

TOM: Hey, Greg! Think about *her* for a change! This is her big moment! What has she done for most of her life? Lie around an apartment. Take an occasional walk at the end of a leash. Give her this, at least. Let her have something to remember.

(They stand watching.)

GREG: That bastard.

TOM: Who? Bowser?

GREG: He raped her.

TOM: Come off it.

GREG: Bowser raped Sylvia!

TOM: She asked for it! She shoved it right in his face!

GREG: *(Grabbing Tom by the shirt.)* Listen, fella. You're talking about my... *(Lets go.)* dog.

TOM: See? See what we're doing? We're thinking of them as people.

GREG: Right.

(They watch.)

GREG: Oh Sylvia...Sylvia...Sylvia...

TOM: After this, you should have her fixed.

GREG: And you should have Bowser neutered.

TOM: Nope. Sorry. It would ruin his personality. There's a major difference between castration and just having your tubes tied, Greg. Think about it.

GREG: *(Poking him in the chest.)* I see. So once again, the women of this world are being asked to suffer the consequences of male aggression. Oh boy, I'm telling you. I'm learning a lot about life these days.

TOM: Cool it, Greg.

(They watch.)

GREG: Do these things always take?

TOM: Not always.

GREG: I almost wish it would.

TOM: Why?

GREG: Sylvia'd make a wonderful mother.

TOM: It's tough having puppies. Particularly in town.

GREG: But I'd be there for her. I'd pitch right in. I'd build a special box for her, with newspapers and a blanket, and get right in there and give a hand. It would give us more in common. Hey, when Kate and I had our kids, I pulled my weight, let me tell you. I helped feed them, and change them, and give them their baths. And on Sunday mornings, we'd bring them into our bed, and we'd all hunker down under the covers. I'd do the same with Sylvia and her pups. Why we'd all...Together we'd...Why, we'd...

(He runs out of steam.)

(Pause.)

TOM: You're sick, man.

GREG: I know it.

TOM: Get her to the vet. First thing.

GREG: *(With a sigh.)* Right.

TOM: And get yourself to a shrink.

GREG: Mmmm.

TOM: *(Looks out.)* Well. *(Watches vicariously.)* Looks like they're done. *(Checks watch.)* Hey. It's late… *(Stretches, flexes, lights a cigarette.)* Come on, Bowser! Let's go, Big Guy! Shake a leg, O Studly One! *(He goes off proudly, smoking.)*

GREG: *(Calling after him.)* You macho bastard!

(Greg kicks the ground angrily. After a moment, Sylvia comes on. Pause. They look at each other.)

GREG: Well, well.

SYLVIA: You speaking to me?

GREG: Have a good time out there?

SYLVIA: I believe it's time to go home.

GREG: I said, did you have a good time?

SYLVIA: I'd prefer not to discuss it. *(Starts off.)*

GREG: Do you like Bowser?

SYLVIA: Who?

GREG: You know damn well who. Bowser. That big guy with his tail up, heading home.

SYLVIA: *(Looking off.)* Oh him.

GREG: Do you like him?

SYLVIA: It's really none of your business, Greg.

GREG: Oh no? Seems to me out there you made it everybody's business.

SYLVIA: Look, Greg. I happen to be exhausted.

GREG: I'll bet you are.

SYLVIA: I am tired, I am hungry, and I am not going to stand around this park discussing ancient history. What happened between me and Bowser is over and done with. It was just a fling, Greg. Just a dumb, silly fling. We both got temporarily carried away. Now let's leave it at that.

GREG: Will it happen again?

SYLVIA: What do you mean?

GREG: Are you still in heat, Sylvia?

SYLVIA: *(Rubbing her back against something.)* I refuse to recognize that expression. I find it somewhat demeaning.

GREG: You are, aren't you?

SYLVIA: I'm not saying I am, I'm not saying I'm not.

GREG: Seems to me a little operation is in order.

SYLVIA: Which means?

GREG: Never mind, but I'm calling the vet first thing.

SYLVIA: That sounds like you plan to punish me.

GREG: No, no.

SYLVIA: It certainly sounds that way.

GREG: It's for your own good.

SYLVIA: Oh yeah, sure. Tell me another.

GREG: I just wish you could exercise a little more self-control.

SYLVIA: May we change the subject, please? May we get on with our lives? *(Taking the leash, handing him his end.)* May we make some attempt to move toward home. I happen to be quite hungry.

GREG: I'll bet you are. Let's go.

(They start off. Suddenly she stops.)

SYLVIA: Hold it.

GREG: What?

SYLVIA: *(Jumping onto the bench.)* Get a load of that dalmatian over there.

GREG: What about him?

SYLVIA: Look at the balls on that guy!

GREG: Let's go, Sylvia.

SYLVIA: On second thought, maybe I want to stay.

GREG: *(Pulling at her.)* Jesus you're a slut, Sylvia. You're a promiscuous slut. It's under the knife for you, kid. First thing.

SYLVIA: You're jealous, aren't you?

GREG: Not at all.

SYLVIA: Yes you are. You're jealous!

GREG: I am not! I just happen to think you can do better, that's all!

SYLVIA: Yeah, yeah, yeah…

(They are off. Music: English Renaissance, possibly Purcell. The apartment. Kate comes on, carrying a document. After a moment, noises are heard off.)

KATE: *(Trying to sound sweet.)* That you, darling?

GREG: *(From off.)* Just us.

KATE: I wonder if we could talk for a minute.

(Greg comes on.)

GREG: Sure. Sure we can talk. *(Calls off.)* Come on, Sylvia.

KATE: Alone, Greg. Without Sylvia.

GREG: She'll be quiet. She's still under the weather, after her operation.

(Sylvia comes in, walking stiff-legged.)

SYLVIA: I feel like a gutted turkey.

GREG: The vet said she'll be shaky for a couple more days.

(Sylvia stands, legs apart, looking at him resentfully.)

SYLVIA: I wish I knew what you had them do to me, you prick.

GREG: *(Low to Kate.)* She's a little mad at me.

KATE: *(Indicating her document.)* Greg, sweetheart, I have some—

GREG: Hold it, dear…Lie down, Sylvia.

SYLVIA: I don't want to lie down.

GREG: Down, Sylvia. *(To Kate.)* She's supposed to lie down. *(To Sylvia.)* Lie down, Sylvia.

(Sylvia, with a sigh, slowly and carefully lies down.)

SYLVIA: Shit. That hurts.

KATE: *(Standing up.)* Greg, I have some very exciting—

GREG: Sit, Kate.

KATE: What?

GREG: Sit down.

KATE: Greg, I am not Sylvia.

GREG: Sorry. I got confused.

KATE: Now. Greg. I have some very exciting news. For both of us.

GREG: Shoot.

KATE: *(Indicating document.)* I got a grant.

GREG: You got a grant?

KATE: To study in England.

GREG: Hey!

KATE: It's from a special foundation set up for women who resume their careers after their child-bearing years.

GREG: *(Hugging her.)* Congratulations, darling! That's fantastic! It's all paying off, isn't it? Those night courses when the kids were growing up. Summer school. It's all coming together.

SYLVIA: *(On the floor; groaning.)* Oooh my gut! My aching gut!

(Greg moves toward Sylvia, Kate tries to keep him focused.)

KATE: So I thought I'd use it to see how the English teach their mother tongue.

GREG: Great idea!

KATE: And…

GREG: And?

KATE: *(Showing him.)* They supply "a spousal supplement."

GREG: A spousal supplement?

KATE: You can come too, darling!

GREG: Fantastic!

KATE: And it couldn't happen at a better time, Greg. With your job in limbo and everything.

SYLVIA: *(Groaning.)* Sweet Jesus, what women go through in this world!

KATE: So I thought we could get a flat in London. And maybe have the kids over for the summer.

GREG: Perfect! *(To Sylvia.)* Hear that, Sylvia? Oh to be in England! Hikes on the moors, kid! *Wuthering Heights? The Hound of the Baskervilles?*

SYLVIA: *(From the floor; groaning.)* Don't talk to me. I'm dying here.

GREG: Just close your eyes and think of England, Sylvia. *(To Kate.)* The English are a great people. They love dogs.

KATE: *(Carefully.)* They do, darling. They definitely do. *(Getting up.)* They love them so much that they're very protective of their own.

GREG: What does that mean?

KATE: They have a quarantine, sweetheart—a six months quarantine—before you can bring a dog into the country.

GREG: That's ridiculous.

KATE: Well they do. I checked, darling. I called the consulate. Even Elizabeth Taylor's dogs were not allowed to set paw on English soil.

GREG: You're saying we can't take Sylvia?

KATE: I'm afraid we can't, sweetheart.

GREG: Those snooty Limey fucks!

KATE: I thought we had an agreement about that word, Greg.

GREG: So Sylvia isn't good enough for them, huh?

KATE: We'll just have to find her a good home, Greg.

> *(Sylvia, on the floor, is now sleeping. She lets out a noisy snore. Greg again moves toward her.)*

KATE: Let sleeping dogs lie, Greg.

GREG: *(Turning to her.)* You applied for this grant, didn't you?

KATE: Of course I applied.

GREG: No, I mean recently. Since Sylvia.

KATE: As a matter of fact, yes.

GREG: And you specifically asked for England.

KATE: English is my field, sweetheart.

GREG: And you knew that Sylvia couldn't come.

KATE: I knew we needed to get away, Greg.

GREG: You are trying to separate me from my dog!

KATE: That's part of it, yes!

GREG: That's a major part of it!

KATE: She's not good for us, Greg! I hate what she does to you and I hate what she does to me! I think— *(She stops.)* What is that awful smell?

GREG: I think it's Sylvia. The vet said she might pass a little gas.

KATE: *(Fanning the air.)* Dammit, Sylvia!

GREG: *(Fanning the air.)* She's had an *operation*, Kate!

KATE: Let's talk about England.

GREG: I don't want to go.

KATE: Greg.

GREG: Not without Sylvia.

KATE: If you loved me, you'd come to England!

GREG: I'll come visit.

KATE: I followed *you* around for twenty years. You can damn well follow me!

GREG: I said I'll visit!

KATE: I plan to be there for six months.

GREG: That long?

KATE: That long.

GREG: I'll last.

KATE: Maybe I *won't,* Greg.

GREG: Are you serious?

KATE: You could find her a home if you wanted to, Greg.

GREG: *This* is her home. This is *my* home.

KATE: Even without me in it?

GREG: I can't give her up, Kate. It's a genetic thing. I have this gene.

KATE: Oh yes? Well I have a gene, too, Greg. It's a gene that tells me I made a major commitment to my mate. It's a gene that reminds me I am responsible for educating my offspring. It's a gene that makes me want to do something constructive about the welfare of the world at large!

(Sylvia lets out another noisy snore. They both look at her.)

GREG: Maybe we should sleep on this one.

KATE: Maybe we should. I'm going to bed. Are you coming?

(Pause.)

GREG: Later.

KATE: This is serious, isn't it?

GREG: I think it is.

KATE: *(To Sylvia.)* Well, Sylvia, thanks a lot. You've managed to chew a huge hole in a twenty-two-year-old marriage!

(Kate goes. Greg stands, looking after her.)

SYLVIA: *(Talking in her sleep, occasionally kicking.)* Hey Bowser! Wait for me, buddy!

GREG: *(Kneeling down beside her.)* Wake up, Sylvia.

SYLVIA: *(Waking up.)* Wumpf. What? Who? Where?

GREG: Time for your pill, kid.

SYLVIA: *(Getting slowly to her feet.)* I hate pills.

GREG: I'll put it in with your food. You won't taste a thing.

SYLVIA: I love you, Greg.

GREG: *(Helping her up.)* I'm a mess, Sylvia.

SYLVIA: I know you are. But even when you behave like a complete asshole, I love you completely.

(They go out slowly together, Sylvia leaning on Greg. Music: possibly Philip Glass. An office with a chair and desk. Venetian blinds. Leslie, a marriage counselor, comes on with Kate. Leslie wears a unisex outfit.)

LESLIE: I must say, Kate, I find it somewhat difficult to counsel married couples when one of the partners refuses to cooperate. I thought your husband agreed to join us.

KATE: He promised he would.

LESLIE: Then let's simply assume he's late.

KATE: Let's simply assume he's with Sylvia…Oh, Leslie. Maybe I should just say the hell with the whole thing!

LESLIE: Now now. Don't give up. We've come a long way, you and I. Please sit, Kate.

KATE: *(Pacing.)* I wish people would stop telling me to sit.

LESLIE: All right, stand, then. But let's take advantage of Greg's absence to review the bidding. *(Consulting her notes.)* During our last session, you seemed to suggest that he had actually fallen in love with Sylvia.

KATE: He has! Totally!

LESLIE: Couldn't you be exaggerating?

KATE: He says things to her that he never says to me!

LESLIE: Such as?

KATE: "You look beautiful, you look wonderful, I love you." All that stuff.

LESLIE: Maybe he is speaking to you *through* Sylvia, Kate. Maybe Sylvia is simply the medium through which he expresses his love for you.

KATE: No, this is different, Leslie. Even when we were first married, he never looked at me the way he looks at Sylvia.

LESLIE: And could you describe that look?

KATE: There's a sort of deep, distant light in his eyes. A sort of…primeval affection.

LESLIE: Do you think…now how shall I put this, Kate?…Do you think there is anything physical in his relationship with Sylvia? Now be frank.

KATE: No!

LESLIE: You're sure? These things happen. There was a couple in here the other day who did very peculiar things with their cat.

KATE: There is nothing physical between Greg and Sylvia. Oh, there's a lot of patting and pawing and stroking and licking—*that* goes on ad nauseam. But nothing beyond that. I almost wish there were.

LESLIE: Why do you say that, Kate?

KATE: Because then it would be just an affair. And any wife worth her salt can deal with that! But this! This is much deeper. I feel I'm up against something that has gone on for hundreds of thousands of years—ever since the first wolf came out of the forest and hunkered down next to the caveman by his fire.

LESLIE: But Kate: Don't you think the cave *woman* must have had ways of shooing that wolf back into outer darkness.

KATE: I've tried! That's why I got the grant to go to England. But all it did was aggravate the issue. Now he loves her even more! He says nothing becomes her like the leaving thereof. So he won't leave her.

(Noise off.)

LESLIE: Ah, but I believe I hear Greg.

(Greg comes in, breathlessly.)

GREG: Sorry I'm late. *(Kisses Kate.)* Hello, darling.

KATE: This is Leslie, Greg.

GREG: *(Shaking hands.)* Hi, Leslie. The reason I'm late is that Sylvia had to have her stitches taken out.

KATE: We're not interested, Greg.

LESLIE: No. Let him talk, Kate. You've had your say, he should have his.

GREG: *(To Leslie.)* While we were at the vet's, we discovered she had worms. *(To Kate, demonstrating.)* Which explains why she's been dragging her butt all over the living room rug. *(To Leslie.)* But we plan to take care of that with little pink pills.

KATE: *(To Leslie.)* See? See what I'm up against?

LESLIE: Kate, why don't you go in the other room and read a magazine. I'd like to talk to Greg alone, if I may.

KATE: Is there a phone out there? Maybe I'll just go ahead and reconfirm my single seat on British Airlines.

LESLIE: *(Ushering her out.)* No, now trust me, Kate. I've been in this business a long, long time.

KATE: But he won't listen. It's impossible to get through. *(Kate goes out.)*

LESLIE: Sit down, Greg.

GREG: Thanks. *(He sits.)*

LESLIE: Talk to me, Greg…Say whatever is on your mind.

GREG: O.K. *(Pause.)* She's not herself lately.

LESLIE: I'm glad you see that, Greg.

GREG: Particularly these past few weeks.

LESLIE: And why do you think that, Greg?

GREG: Oh I know exactly why. She resents me.

LESLIE: And why do you suppose she resents you?

GREG: Because I made the decision.

LESLIE: What decision?

GREG: To have her spayed.

LESLIE: Ah…You're talking about…

GREG: Sylvia.

LESLIE: Sylvia.

GREG: You don't want me to talk about Sylvia?

LESLIE: No I do. If you want to, Greg.

GREG: Kate doesn't like me to.

LESLIE: Well that's Kate, Greg. As for me, I'd like very much to hear about Sylvia. Because by telling me about Sylvia, you are really telling me about yourself.

GREG: O.K. Well, to begin with, she's got great eyes.

LESLIE: Sylvia?

GREG: Sylvia. I finally understand the word "limpid" now. She's got limpid eyes. Limpid, deep, serious eyes. But that doesn't mean she's serious all the time. She laughs. I've actually seen her laugh. And she's got this great little butt. Everyone comments on her butt. When she sashays down the street, she kind of wiggles it back and forth. A lot of people stop to pat her, just because of that butt. And when we get to the park, the whole gang goes nuts for her. Even though she's been spayed, they gather around. You should see Bowser, for example—oh and hey, I found this poem that Shakespeare wrote about her.

LESLIE: Shakespeare?

GREG: *(Recites.)*

"Who is Sylvia? What is she,
That all our swains commend her?…"

LESLIE: Greg.

GREG: "Holy, fair, and wise is she…"

LESLIE: Greg!

GREG: "The heavens such grace did—"

LESLIE: GREG!

GREG: Yes?

LESLIE: I'm afraid we're confined to the fifty-minute hour.

GREG: Sorry. I get carried away.

LESLIE: *(Leaving the desk, standing in front of him.)* Greg, I'm going to do something here which I normally do much further along in the therapy process. I'm going to put myself into the picture.

GREG: Yourself?

LESLIE: What's my name, Greg?

GREG: Kate said it was Leslie.

LESLIE: Leslie it is, Greg. Now am I a man or a woman?

GREG: You're a… *(Hesitates.)* Woman.

LESLIE: You hesitated, Greg.

GREG: Yes. Well. Sorry.

LESLIE: No, no. I wanted you to hesitate. I wanted you to select my gender. That's why I call myself Leslie. It's a name which works either way.

GREG: It does, doesn't it?

LESLIE: And that's why I wear these ambivalent clothes. I may be a man pretending to be a woman, or I may be a woman pretending to be a man. I let my patients select my gender, Greg.

GREG: I thought you were a woman.

LESLIE: Because you wanted me to be a woman.

GREG: I did?

LESLIE: We project our needs onto the world, Greg. Life is shapeless and absurd. We use words, names, and categories to give us a sense of shape. We need that sense of shape to get through the day.

GREG: O.K.

LESLIE: You even see it in the Bible, Greg. God has Adam name the animals. So that Adam can construct his own order out of the chaos around him.

GREG: Hmmm.

LESLIE: Which brings us to your dog, Greg.

GREG: Sylvia.

LESLIE: Sylvia. You wanted your dog to be a woman, too. That's why you named her Sylvia.

GREG: She was already named Sylvia.

LESLIE: But you embraced the name. Because you needed a woman.

GREG: I already have a woman. Her name is Kate.

LESLIE: *(Becoming impatient.)* You wanted another kind of woman, Greg. You wanted the subservient little wife you once kept in the suburbs. You wanted the worshipful daughter who once hung on your every word. You wanted a Sylvia, Greg. If Sylvia didn't exist, you would have had to invent her.

GREG: You may be right, Leslie.

LESLIE: *(Sardonically.)* I think I am, Greg. *(All business.)* Now these are what we therapists call "the dangerous years."

GREG: The dangerous years.

LESLIE: The years between the first hint of retirement and the first whiff of the nursing home.

GREG: Oh God.

LESLIE: No, we should make the most of these years, Greg. I, for example, am exploring the boundaries of gender identification. Kate is moving beyond child rearing to a career in the public classroom. You, on the other hand, seem to have retreated into a kind of pastoral nostalgia.

GREG: Pastoral nostalgia?

LESLIE: By acquiring Sylvia.

GREG: You think that's true?

LESLIE: I do, Greg. And I think it's time to move on. It's time for you to accept the challenges that come with later life.

GREG: Maybe so.

LESLIE: Drop the leash, Greg, and once again take hold of your wife's hand. See if you are capable of walking with her, side by side, toward the setting sun.

GREG: Thank you, Leslie. This all makes a lot of sense.

LESLIE: I think it does, Greg. I think it makes a great deal of sense. *(Gets up, stretches.)* I must say I'm exhausted. This has been a long, tough haul for all of us. *(Smiles.)* Well. Now may I bring in Kate so we can all sit down together and work through a few specifics.

GREG: Aren't you forgetting one thing?

LESLIE: What thing, Greg.

GREG: Sylvia.

LESLIE: Sylvia?

GREG: You've seen Kate, you've seen me, don't you think you should see Sylvia?

LESLIE: You want me to hold a session with your dog?

GREG: Not a *session*, Leslie! Jesus, what kind of a nut case do you think I am? No, I just think you should pat her, maybe play with her a little, possibly take her for a short walk. Because then you'll see, Leslie…

LESLIE: See what?

GREG: Then you'll see that Sylvia is more than just a name, or a gene, or a psychological symptom, or anything else that tries to pin her down. Any dog-owner knows this. If you don't, Leslie, you should get one immediately. We should all have dogs. It should be put in the constitution. It's not just a right, it's an obligation. When you register to vote, you pick up your dog license. The world would be a far better place, Leslie. Why just think: You and I and Nelson Mandela and Yassir Arafat and Meryl

Streep could all meet at Club Med or someplace, and what would we talk about? Our dogs, Leslie! Our dogs.

(Long pause.)

LESLIE: *(Quietly.)* Greg.

GREG: Yes?

LESLIE: Greg, I'd like you to leave right now. Quickly, if you would. And send Kate in on your way out.

GREG: *(Looks at watch.)* It's Sylvia's dinnertime, anyway.

(Hurries out, as Kate comes back in.)

KATE: What hap—

LESLIE: Kate, I want you to do several things.

KATE: Several…?

LESLIE: First I want you to divorce Greg.

KATE: Divorce—?

LESLIE: Take him for every nickel he's got!

KATE: Oh I couldn't—

LESLIE: Then I want you to get a gun.

KATE: A gun?

LESLIE: To shoot Sylvia. I hope you get her right between the eyes.

KATE: But…

LESLIE: Sorry. I'm late for my shrink. *(Exits quickly, tearing up the case folder.)*

KATE: *(Remaining; to herself.)* "If this were played on the stage now, I would condemn it as an improbable fiction." *Twelfth Night.* Act Three. *(She exits.)* *(Music: possibly Vera Lynn singing "Now is the Hour." The apartment. Greg enters with Sylvia. She is now wearing a very attractive little black dress.)*

GREG: *(Taking the leash out of her hand.)* You look particularly glamorous today, Sylvia.

SYLVIA: Thank you, Greg.

GREG: You know why, don't you?

SYLVIA: Tell me, while I check out *le kibble du jour. (She goes off.)*

GREG: *(Calling after her.)* You look particularly glamorous because we've come to a major moment in our relationship.

SYLVIA: *(Returning.)* A major moment?

GREG: A turning point. And at turning points in our lives, good or bad, we instinctively shine. Our eyes sparkle, our hair glistens, our bodies seem to know.

SYLVIA: But why is this a turning point?

GREG: We're going to lay our cards on the table. Both of us.

SYLVIA: I thought we always did that anyway.

GREG: We did. We do. But this will be even more so. Up until now, you've been saying what I hoped you'd say. This time, I want you to feel you're totally on your own.

SYLVIA: Sounds exciting.

GREG: Would you like to sit down, Sylvia.

SYLVIA: *(Slyly.)* Where shall I sit?

GREG: Anywhere you want.

SYLVIA: Can I sit on the couch?

GREG: You may, Sylvia. Come on. I'll even give you a hand. *(He helps her onto the couch.)*

SYLVIA: *(Making a big deal of it.)* Dis is da life! I like these major moments, Greg.

GREG: Sylvia, I have to send you away.

SYLVIA: Away?

GREG: To somewhere else.

SYLVIA: Oh you mean that kennel you put me in when you went off on that weekend? I can live with that. As long as it's just a few days.

GREG: It's not a kennel, Sylvia. I've found a family for you.

SYLVIA: Fine. Sounds better than a kennel.

GREG: And it won't be for just a few days.

SYLVIA: How long will it be? Two weeks? Three?

GREG: Forever, Sylvia.

SYLVIA: Forever?

GREG: It boils down to you or Kate, Sylvia. And I'm choosing Kate.

SYLVIA: You're choosing *Kate?*

GREG: I have to, Sylvia.

SYLVIA: You can't have us both?

GREG: I guess I can't.

SYLVIA: *(Leaving the couch.)* Is this because she hates me?

GREG: She doesn't *hate* you, Sylvia.

SYLVIA: She sure doesn't like me.

GREG: She doesn't like *me,* Sylvia. When I'm with you.

SYLVIA: Lord knows I've tried to please her.

GREG: You have, Sylvia.

SYLVIA: I always greet her when she comes home.

GREG: I know that.

SYLVIA: She seems to like it when I lick the plates before they go in the dishwasher. She even encourages the habit.

GREG: That's only because she doesn't like waste, Sylvia.

SYLVIA: So you're choosing her over me.

GREG: She's my wife, Sylvia. She's the mother of my children. We've lived together a long, long time.

SYLVIA: Do you love her?

GREG: I do. Very much.

SYLVIA: I thought you loved me.

GREG: I do, sweetheart. But in a different way. And it's not a good way, as far as Kate is concerned.

SYLVIA: I thought there was talk of you and me moving out.

GREG: There was.

SYLVIA: I thought there was serious talk of you and me getting a studio apartment over on 69th Street, right near the park.

GREG: There was talk of that, yes, Sylvia. In the heat of the moment.

SYLVIA: I thought we were going to take a camping trip on Chesapeake Bay. I thought you were going to teach me to retrieve ducks.

GREG: I was going to do all that, Sylvia.

SYLVIA: And you've suddenly chickened out?

GREG: That's what I've done. Chickened out.

(Pause.)

SYLVIA: I feel awful.

GREG: So do I.

SYLVIA: Know what I wish I could do? Mix myself a double Absolut vodka on the rocks with a twist.

GREG: I did that earlier, Sylvia. For myself.

SYLVIA: Yeah, well, being a dog, I don't happen to have the solace of alcohol, Greg.

GREG: *(Reaching into his jacket pocket.)* I've got a Bark Bar for you.

SYLVIA: A what?

GREG: A Bark Bar. Remember? I bought you one on our last walk over to the East Side. You loved it. *(He holds it out.)*

SYLVIA: *(Taking it, looking it over.)* It's in the shape of a cat.

GREG: I thought you'd be amused by that.

SYLVIA: Amused? Amused by those fuckers? *(Takes a bite.)* Not bad. *(Chews.)* But not good enough. *(Sits in the chair.)* Tell me about this family you're shipping me off to.

GREG: *(Kneeling beside her.)* They're great, Sylvia. I advertised in the Westchester newspapers. I interviewed a number of applicants.

SYLVIA: Thanks for letting me in on it.

GREG: You'll be living in the suburbs, Sylvia.

SYLVIA: I hate the suburbs.

GREG: What? All that green grass? This family has half an acre, all fenced in.

SYLVIA: That Akita in the park used to live in the suburbs. He said you're totally alone out there. There's no sense of being part of a pack. And if you try to meet someone by taking a walk, there's a good chance you'll get run over.

GREG: You won't want to take walks, Sylvia. You'll want to stay close to home.

SYLVIA: Why?

GREG: Because you'll like this family so much.

SYLVIA: Why?

GREG: Well, for one thing, they have children.

SYLVIA: How many?

GREG: Three.

SYLVIA: Any babies?

GREG: One.

SYLVIA: I hate babies.

GREG: You don't, Sylvia. You're always licking their faces.

SYLVIA: Their mouths taste good, but they're always stepping on your tail.

GREG: Well there are also two teenagers, Sylvia. They're eager to have you. They want to teach you to play Frisbee. They want to take you to Little League games. They'll be much better for you than I could possibly be.

SYLVIA: I hate teenagers.

GREG: You don't.

SYLVIA: (Getting up.) I do. I hate them. They're totally unreliable. They forget to feed you. They play music which hurts your ears. One minute they're showering you with love, then they leave you locked in some car for hours on end— (Throwing herself on him.) Oh Greg, don't do this to me! Please! Don't send me away! Keep me here with you! Please!

GREG: I can't.

SYLVIA: I'll change, Greg. I'll change my ways. I'll stop chewing shoes. I'll bring Kate the New York *Times* every morning—well I won't do that, that's too corny—but I'll do something else! Just tell me what to do, and I'll do it!

GREG: I promised Kate I'd give you away, Sylvia. I made that promise. To my wife.

SYLVIA: When?

GREG: Today.

SYLVIA: To*day*?

GREG: I'm driving you out right now.

SYLVIA: Can't I even say good-bye to Bowser?

GREG: You just saw him in the park.

SYLVIA: Jesus, you're something, Greg. You really are. You bring me home, you get me all dependent on you, you spay me…

GREG: Sylvia…

SYLVIA: You had me *spayed*, Greg! You destroyed my womanhood. And then, when I get over that, when I still decide that the sun rises and sets only in your direction, then suddenly you're packing me off to some boring nuclear family in Westchester county. Christ, Greg! Don't you feel guilty about this?

GREG: I do, Sylvia. I feel terrible.

SYLVIA: I mean, shit. You have a moral obligation here! What would the Humane Society say about this? How would they react at the A.S.P.C.A.?

GREG: They'd say I'm doing the right thing!

SYLVIA: Bullshit! That's just bullshit, Greg!

GREG: They'd say that a week out there with your new family, and you'll forget all about me.

SYLVIA: Never!

GREG: Sure you will. If I came out to visit you, you might run up for a pat and a sniff, but that would be that.

SYLVIA: You're so wrong, Greg! You're so goddamn wrong! Read the *Odyssey* some time. That guy was gone for twenty years, and when he finally got home, the first person to recognize him—before his nurse, before his son, before his own *wife*, goddammit—was his dog! That dog was lying outside the palace for all those years, waiting for him, Greg. Lying on a dung heap just waiting for his master. And when his master finally showed, what did the dog do? He raised his head, wagged his tail, and died.

GREG: *(Hugging her.)* Oh don't, Sylvia!

SYLVIA: I'll never forget you, Greg! Ever!

GREG: Stop, Sylvia! Please! I can't stand this.

SYLVIA: Well. *(She finishes her biscuit.)* Let's get it over with. *(She gets up, takes his arm à la Blanche Dubois.)* I'll have to depend on the kindness of strangers…Take me to the suburbs. I hope I can at least sit next to you on the front seat. After all, her majesty won't be there to object.
(Kate's voice is heard from offstage.)

KATE: *(From off.)* Hello!

SYLVIA: Or will she?

GREG: What's she doing home?

SYLVIA: Christ! I feel like sneaking off and hiding under some bed!
(She goes off. Kate comes on.)

GREG: I thought you had a meeting.

KATE: It broke up early.

GREG: We're just getting ready to go.

KATE: Where's Saliva?

GREG: Sylvia, Kate.

KATE: Where is she?

GREG: At the moment, I imagine she's trying to stay out of your hair. *(Starts off.)*

KATE: Greg.

GREG: What?

KATE: I know this is hard for you.

GREG: Damn right.

KATE: I want you to know I appreciate it.

GREG: Thanks.

KATE: We'll have a good time in England, Greg. It will be a whole new thing.

GREG: I can't talk about it, Kate. It's too painful at the moment. *(Starts off again.)*

KATE: Do you plan to take all her stuff?

GREG: They're in a bag in the front hall.

KATE: Her bed? Her brush? Her kibble dish?

GREG: They're all there.

KATE: What about her little red ball?

GREG: I can't find it.

KATE: *(Looking under a couch pillow.)* She liked that little red ball.

GREG: At least you noticed.

KATE: It's a shame to send her off without it.

GREG: She'll survive. *(He starts off again.)*

KATE: Actually, my meeting is still going on, Greg. I ducked out early.

GREG: Oh yes?

KATE: I thought I should come home and say good-bye.

GREG: *(Sarcastically.)* To Saliva?

KATE: To Sylvia.

GREG: Why?

KATE: I wanted to.

GREG: Magnanimous in victory, eh?

KATE: Greg…

GREG: Well. Have your farewell scene. *(Calls.)* Sylvia! Come! *(Pause.)* I don't think she wants to. *(Calls again.)* Sylvia!
(Sylvia comes on reluctantly, now dressed in the scruffy outfit she was first found in.)

SYLVIA: *(Sarcastically.)* You called, massa?

GREG: Kate wants to say good-bye to you.

SYLVIA: Oh sure. And I'm Marie of Rumania. *(Starts off again.)*

KATE: Come here, Sylvia.

SYLVIA: *(To Greg.)* Who's she kidding?

KATE: *(Holding out her arms.)* Sylvia. Come.

GREG: Go on, Sylvia. She's human. Say good-bye.

    (Sylvia crosses warily to Kate. Kate embraces her while Sylvia stands stiffly.)

KATE: Sylvia, I know it's been tough sledding between you and me, but I do want to say good-bye.

SYLVIA: *(Over her shoulder, to Greg.)* What is this? Some sudden sisterhood thing?

GREG: Easy now.

KATE: I wish…I wish it could have been otherwise, Sylvia.

SYLVIA: *(Breaking away.)* So do I, and now can I go? *(She goes to Greg.)*

GREG: We'll be off then. Kate.

KATE: Good-bye, Sylvia.

SYLVIA: *(Over her shoulder.)* Yeah, yeah.

    (Sylvia and Greg go out.)

KATE: *(Standing, calling after them.)* Greg, you should at least stop at the pet store, and get her another little red—

    (Sylvia comes back on, carrying a paperback. She drops it at Kate's feet.)

SYLVIA: I hear you've been looking for this.

KATE: *(Picking it up.)* My *All's Well That Ends Well!*

SYLVIA: Whatever.

KATE: *(Looking it over.)* And it's in reasonably good shape, Sylvia. There's just one little chew mark here on the corner.

    (Sylvia sings defiantly, à la Piaf something like "Je ne Regrette Rien." Greg comes back on.)

GREG: She found it in the hall closet, and insisted on bringing it right in.

KATE: *You* found it, Greg. And sent her in with it.

GREG: Suit yourself, Kate…I'll call the garage. *(He goes out.)*

SYLVIA: *(Over her shoulder to Greg.)* I'll be right with you.

GREG: *(As he goes.)* O.K.

SYLVIA: *(To Kate.)* I've been thinking about what you said.

KATE: What I said?

SYLVIA: "I wish it could have been otherwise." I've been thinking about that. Know what "otherwise" is, Kate? Otherwise is that man who ran off with his grandchildren's au pair. Or that guy who took a shot at his wife while she was doing her step aerobics. Otherwise is those sad couples sitting in restaurants night after night, eyeing each other, with absolutely nothing to say. That's otherwise, Kate.

KATE: Is it, Sylvia?

SYLVIA: Yes, and I'll tell you what "this wise" is. "This wise" is the fact that he can never be happy with me unless you like me, too. Which is why he is always foisting me on you. Which is called sharing, Kate. Which is what some people sometimes call love. That's "this wise," Kate.

GREG: *(From off.)* O.K., Sylvia. Let's go.

SYLVIA: Of course what do I know? I'm only a dog. *(She goes off.)*

(The sound of a door closing offstage. Kate looks after them. Music begins softly underneath, the majestic, slowly building Tuba Mirum section of the Dies Irae from Verdi's Requiem. Kate stands and thinks. Then she goes and sits in the chair, begins to thumb through her book. Something makes her uncomfortable. The music builds. She shifts her position. She reaches under the cushion, retrieves Sylvia's little red ball. She clasps it, then holds it aloft triumphantly while the music begins to come to a climax. She rises majestically, strides to the doorway as the music reaches its crescendo, then stops. A moment.)

KATE: *(To herself.)* Oh hell. As Shakespeare once said, "What the fuck."

(She goes off determinedly after Greg and Sylvia. Greg comes on quickly from the opposite side as the lights focus on him.)

GREG: *(To audience.)* We never got to the suburbs. I called and said we'd changed our minds. The folks understood, of course. Being dog lovers like ourselves.

(Kate comes back on.)

KATE: *(To audience.)* And I changed my mind about England. Oh I went— for a few weeks. But for the most part, I stayed here. While Greg looked around for another job.

GREG: *(To audience.)* And Sylvia stayed. She stayed with us for the next eleven years, until everything went wrong with her and we had to put her down. I held her when the vet gave her the shot. She looked at me, gave a little sigh, lay down quietly, and died. *(Pause.)* Kate was waiting for me when I got home, and we both cried.

KATE: *(To audience.)* That's not true. I did not cry.

GREG: You did. You just won't admit it.

KATE: *(To audience.)* Sylvia and I never really liked each other. Even later on.

GREG: You got along famously.

KATE: *(To audience.)* We tolerated each other. If that.

GREG: *(To audience.)* Once I came home from my new job with Wildlife

Conservation International...and found Kate and Sylvia side by side on the couch.

KATE: *(To audience.)* This is an absolute lie!

GREG: *(To audience.)* Kate was reading *The Hidden Life of Dogs,* and Sylvia had her head in Kate's lap.

KATE: *(To audience.)* This is a total male fantasy!

GREG: *(To audience.)* I'll also tell you something else. Over the years a strange thing happened. Sylvia and I didn't talk so much.

KATE: *(To audience.)* Now this *is* true.

GREG: Oh we *talked.* But less and less. It was as if we learned to understand each other *without* talking. Or maybe we learned that we could never understand each other.

KATE: *(Coming close to him, taking his arm.)* Or maybe it was because you and I talked more.

GREG: Whatever. *(To audience.)* But Sylvia's looks changed too.

KATE: *(To audience.)* They did. She began to look...well, different. *(To Greg.)* Show them the picture.

GREG: *(To audience.)* I'll show you Sylvia's picture. *(He takes out his wallet, opens it, displays a small color photograph. Behind, we see a large, appealing blown-up photograph of an ordinary dog.)* There. That's Sylvia.

KATE: *(To audience.)* I took that picture the year before she died.

GREG: *(To audience.)* Note who took it.

KATE: *(To Greg as they look at their picture.)* I'm afraid she looks a little the worse for wear.

GREG: She does not, Kate! She still looks absolutely gorgeous! *(Affectionately.)* Ah Sylvia!

KATE: *(With a sigh.)* Oh Sylvia.

(The lights fade on Greg and Kate, very much together, looking at Sylvia's picture. Behind them, the large photo of Sylvia stays lit a little longer. Music comes up, possibly the Benny Goodman Quartet rendition of "Ev'ry Time We Say Good-bye.")

THE END

LABOR DAY

*To Jack O'Brien
with great affection and appreciation*

INTRODUCTION

This play is very close to my own bones. I wrote it to dramatize the conflict I have always felt between my love for my own family and my commitment to the "families" that come out of the collaborative experiences in theatre. I return here to the character of John, who was in my play *The Cocktail Hour,* trying to write about his parents. In *Labor Day,* he hopes to bring it all together by writing about his children and grandchildren.

With this play, I had my usual good luck in having a top-notch director, Jack O'Brien, and a fine cast, and the hospitable venue of the Old Globe Theatre in San Diego to try things out. The local response was encouraging, but there was a hint of trouble on the horizon when the Los Angeles critic summarily dismissed us. Since the play was a co-production with the Manhattan Theatre Club, we moved on to New York, where we opened to a general chorus of disapproval. I'm still not sure why. Maybe the play is too cozy and self-reflexive for these edgy times. Maybe the element in its plot that depends on snagging a notoriously unavailable Hollywood star is irritating and implausible. And maybe the play simply doesn't have enough of what the TV people call a "jeopardy element."

The theme of family and continuity doesn't seem to resonate with today's audiences, particularly when "family values" now have such reductive political connotations. *Life with Father,* a huge success in its day, isn't revived much these days, and even on television, the concerns of family life have modulated into the very different conflicts and anxieties of the workplace. Parents, let alone grandparents, occasionally get guest spots, but they certainly don't preside over the scene. By setting *Labor Day* in the study of a writer who has patriarchal delusions, I tried to pull together and combine the elements of home and work. It's where I was when I wrote the play, and where I still am, but I guess many people these days would rather be somewhere else.

ORIGINAL PRODUCTION

Labor Day was first produced by the Old Globe Theatre (Jack O'Brien, Artistic Director; Tom Hall, Managing Director) in San Diego, California, on February 12, 1998. The production was subsequently transferred to the Manhattan Theatre Club (Lynn Meadow, Artistic Director; Barry Grove, Executive Director) in New York City, on June 1, 1998. It was directed by Jack O'Brien; the set design was by Ralph Funicello; the costume design was by Michael Krass; the lighting design was by Kenneth Posner; and the sound design was by Jeff Ladman. In San Diego, the production stage manager was Lurie Pfeffer; in New York it was Denise Yaney. The cast was as follows:

Ellen . . . . Joyce Van Patten
Dennis . . . . Brooks Ashmanskas
John. . . . . Josef Sommer
Ralph. . . . . James Colby
Ginny. . . . . Veanne Cox

CHARACTERS

ELLEN: older
DENNIS: younger
JOHN: older
RALPH: younger
GINNY: younger

SETTING

A writer's "studio" in Connecticut, a couple of hours northeast of New York City. The studio, set apart from a nearby farm house, was once a chicken coop, and hints of its origins can be seen in the whitewashed walls of rough-hewn boards, and the roosting cubicles that now contain books, manuscripts, records and tapes, all casually organized. On the walls are a number of framed posters of plays, along with photos from different productions. On a shelf there might be a model of a set, and somewhere else a dartboard, surrounded by yellowing newspaper and magazine reviews and photos of critics. Upstage, windows open out on an expansive view of rolling farmland.

The studio is furnished with a commodious desk on which are scattered reference books, papers, and an old mechanical typewriter. A swivel chair on casters is placed in front of it. The studio also contains a reading chair with a footstool, table, and reading lamp, along with a small refrigerator, an old coffeemaker, and a few chipped cups. A door opens onto a pathway leading to the main house, which is a short distance away.

TIME

Labor Day; today.

ACT I

At rise: The studio is empty. The sounds of kids and games are heard coming through the screen door. We hear voices approaching;. Ellen and Dennis come in. Ellen is a tan, good-looking, older woman, wearing informal summer clothes. Dennis is in his early thirties. He is paler, wears funky city clothes and carries a large shoulder bag.

ELLEN: *(As they enter)* Here we are.

DENNIS: *(Looking around.)* Great place to write.

ELLEN: It was originally a chicken coop.

DENNIS: This?

ELLEN: When the children were born, he kicked out the chickens, and moved in his typewriter.

DENNIS: Cool.

ELLEN: Lately he's been saying…never mind. I don't know you well enough.

DENNIS: Hey, please. I'm a big boy.

ELLEN: He's been saying that over the years, it has continued to produce primarily chickenshit.

DENNIS: He's wrong.

ELLEN: Of course he's wrong.

DENNIS: I've read all his plays.

ELLEN: Good for you.

DENNIS: And directed four of them.

ELLEN: Four! Good heavens. Where?

DENNIS: The first when I was still in college. Then a revival off-off-*off* Broadway. And two in the regional theatres.

ELLEN: Which ones?

DENNIS: *Love in Buffalo* and *Saint Jane.*

ELLEN: Uh-oh…Did you get them to work?

DENNIS: I did.

ELLEN: Good for you. And good for the regional theatres.

DENNIS: This will be the first time I've directed a new one.

ELLEN: What new one?

DENNIS: His new play.

ELLEN: What new play?

DENNIS: Hasn't he told you?

ELLEN: He has not.

DENNIS: His own wife?

ELLEN: I didn't think it was finished.

DENNIS: It isn't, actually. It needs work.

ELLEN: You plan to make him rewrite it?

DENNIS: That's why I'm here.

ELLEN: Oh lord. He'll be thrashing around all night. I'll have to move into the guest room.

DENNIS: No sweat. This should be easy for him.

ELLEN: Why do you think he smuggled it past me?

DENNIS: Who knows?

ELLEN: Is it some bitter indictment of married life?

DENNIS: Not at all.

ELLEN: I love bitter indictments of married life.

DENNIS: This is just the opposite.

ELLEN: Damn. How about some coffee? *(Glancing out.)* He should be back any minute.

DENNIS: Thanks.

(Ellen makes coffee, using bottled water. She finds a cup, wipes out the dust, as if she's done this many times before.)

DENNIS: Hey look, I feel bad showing up on your doorstep this way. I mean, Labor Day and all. I kept trying to call but the line was always busy.

ELLEN: The kids have been on the phone all weekend.

DENNIS: Actually, I need to talk to him face-to-face. So I rented a car and drove up.

ELLEN: That's very enterprising.

DENNIS: I get a deal for half a day.

(Noise from outside.)

DENNIS: Quite a gang out there.

ELLEN: Today you get the complete cast of characters.

DENNIS: Could you break it down for me?

ELLEN: I'll give you the broad outlines. First, our four children. That's for openers.

DENNIS: Four!

ELLEN: All two years apart.

DENNIS: Talk about a baby boom.

ELLEN: Then we discovered what was causing it.

(Dennis looks at her.)

ELLEN: That's a line from one of his plays.

DENNIS: I know…So go on. Four children and…?

ELLEN: And three spouses. Plus one significant concubine. Six grandchildren, one au pair from Lithuania, two dogs, and one partially house-trained puppy.

DENNIS: I suppose you've got everything planned.

ELLEN: Planned? Planned. Oh, I guess there's some vague underlying structure. Last night, for example, we had our final cookout. It ended with
somebody getting sick. This morning, we have the annual tennis match—
sons against sons-in-law—which will end with somebody getting mad.
And then the last swim for the kids, with somebody getting cold.
Somewhere along the line we'll have what was once called lunch. You're
welcome to partake, Dennis.

DENNIS: Thanks. If I'm still around.

ELLEN: *(As she continues to make the coffee.)* Milk? Sugar?

DENNIS: Both, thanks.

*(Ellen sniffs a carton of milk in the refrigerator, finds it is sour, puts it aside,
discovers a relatively fresher one.)*

ELLEN: After lunch, there will be a series of ritual arguments about who takes
a nap and who doesn't. Then a whiffle-ball game for all ages, which is a
little like the croquet game in *Alice in Wonderland:* The rules change constantly, the bases move around, and everyone ends up vaguely unhappy.

DENNIS: Sounds like the Tony Awards.

ELLEN: Exactly! And then we all say good-bye, because school starts tomorrow and people go back to work.

DENNIS: No wonder they call this Labor Day.

ELLEN: Well, the dogs clean up. And the kids pitch in. Or try to. My daughter Ginny is always a huge help.

(Dennis laughs.)

ELLEN: What.

DENNIS: *(Laughing.)* I just thought. This is kind of funny.

ELLEN: What is?

DENNIS: This. You and me, standing around, setting the scene. It's like the beginning of one of his plays.

ELLEN: *(Handing him his coffee.)* They say life imitates art.

DENNIS: That's true. Wagner wrote *Tristan and Isolde,* and only afterwards
decided to commit adultery.

ELLEN: Is the new play about adultery?

DENNIS: No.

ELLEN: Some married man doesn't fall in love with some bumptuous bimbo?

DENNIS: God, no.

ELLEN: How about some married woman? Does she go to bed with some gorgeous male?

DENNIS: No way.

ELLEN: Damn. Sounds a little boring.

DENNIS: Not if I work it right.

(Increased family sounds offstage.)

DENNIS: Noises off.

ELLEN: Sounds like he's back… *(Goes to door, calls out.)* John! You've got a visitor!

(Children's voices. John's voice is heard over them.)

JOHN'S VOICE: All right now, gang. Look what I've got! Three Heath Bar Crunch ice cream bars and one Chunky Monkey.

(Cheers.)

JOHN'S VOICE: Who wants the Chunky Monkey?

(A chorus of demands.)

ELLEN: *(To Dennis.)* He used to come back with the *New York Times*. Now he comes laden with empty calories.

DENNIS: So does the *New York Times*.

(John comes in, informally dressed. He is about Ellen's age.)

JOHN: So who's here?

DENNIS: Me, John.

JOHN: Dennis! Well, well.

(Children's voices continue.)

JOHN: Excuse me. *(Toward off as he goes.)* O.K., O.K., no arguing, please! We'll raffle off the Chunky Monkey! How many fingers do I have behind my back?

(He is off. Children's noises slowly subside.)

ELLEN: Dennis, one thing I care very much about is his nap.

DENNIS: His nap.

ELLEN: After lunch. When the little ones go down, so does he. I'm ruthless about that.

DENNIS: But he said he was all right.

ELLEN: He's in remission.

DENNIS: But that's good, isn't it?

ELLEN: He has a checkup tomorrow. We've all got our fingers crossed.

DENNIS: He seemed very cheery when we spoke last.

ELLEN: Oh he is. He keeps saying this whole ordeal made him feel very lucky.

DENNIS: Lucky?

ELLEN: He says we're all in remission, all the time. And he's lucky enough to realize it…

(John comes on again.)

JOHN: So! Dennis! Is that your purple Dodge Intrepid crouched in our drive-way, ready to spring?

DENNIS: Just rented, John.

JOHN: Glad to hear it.

ELLEN: I didn't know you had finished your play, John.

JOHN: Just recently, darling.

ELLEN: How come I haven't read it?

JOHN: I wanted a little feedback first.

ELLEN: I thought feedback began at home.

JOHN: Sweetheart, I'm not sure Dennis here is interested in our timeworn domestic rituals.

ELLEN: Do you poke fun at people in this one?

JOHN: Poke fun?

ELLEN: Needle then? Make digs?

JOHN: Of course not.

ELLEN: I don't believe you. *(To Dennis.)* This man is dangerous, Dennis. He can hurt.

JOHN: Trust me on this one, darling.

ELLEN: I don't, but I'll get out of your hair.

JOHN: If it ever grows back.

ELLEN: You've got more than you had before.

JOHN: You keep saying that.

ELLEN: Because it's true.

(She goes. Family noises from outside.)

JOHN: *(To Dennis.)* So. Dennis. You have tracked me to my lair. What do you think of my native habitat?

DENNIS: I think you're running a fucking day-care center.

JOHN: I like to call it a small farm. Away from Rome. And the din of the Coliseum.

DENNIS: Yeah right.

JOHN: A few acres of stony New England soil. A vegetable garden, hand-tilled by yours truly. A couple of horses in the barn, owned and maintained by a good neighbor. And a Vietnamese pot-bellied pig for the grandchildren.

DENNIS: I like your chicken coop.

JOHN: It's good for producing chickenshit.

DENNIS: Stop saying that.

JOHN: What do you mean? I only said it once.

DENNIS: According to your wife, you say it all the time.

JOHN: Now see? That's the trouble with being married so long. Your wife steals all your best lines.

DENNIS: It's a lousy line anyway. I'd cut it. *(Looking at him.)* You look good, by the way.

JOHN: Thanks. I actually played a quick set of singles with my son Ralph earlier this morning. I lost, of course. But I comfort myself with the thought that there's one greater pleasure than beating one's own son. And that's losing to him.

DENNIS: Put that in a play.

JOHN: I already have…You look good, too, Dennis.

DENNIS: Thanks.

JOHN: No, actually you don't. You look pale.

DENNIS: I've been working. All summer. I did a *Three Sisters* in San Francisco, followed immediately by a *Coriolanus* in Louisville.

JOHN: *Coriolanus* on top of *The Three Sisters?* How'd he do?

DENNIS: Who?

JOHN: Never mind. It must feel good to get home.

DENNIS: What's home?

JOHN: I thought you bought an apartment in New York. With your lighting designer.

DENNIS: We'll probably have to give it up.

JOHN: Why?

DENNIS: Because we're never there. Jason's lighting a sitcom in LA. He's been asked to stay on.

JOHN: The siren song of Los Angeles.

DENNIS: He's making up his mind this weekend. Which is thoughtful of him, seeing as how our next mortgage payment comes due tomorrow.

JOHN: Lots of things come due tomorrow.

DENNIS: The theatre's a shitty place to maintain a relationship.

JOHN: It's not easy.

(Sounds from outside.)

JOHN: I liked Jason, by the way.

DENNIS: So did I. *(Opening his bag.)* But. On with the show. We've got good news. John. *(Takes out script.)* Very good news. *(Kisses the script.)* Almost the best.

JOHN: Ah, then in heaven's name pray put me in possession of it.

DENNIS: What's that from?

JOHN: *Oliver Twist.* I've been reading Dickens.

DENNIS: The Seattle Rep wants to do this in November. On their main stage.

JOHN: My agent said they might be interested.

DENNIS: *Might* be *in*terested? They flipped for it, John! They called Thursday afternoon.

JOHN: Why didn't they call *me?*

DENNIS: They tried. Get call waiting, John.

JOHN: It's rude. I was brought up never to interrupt.

DENNIS: They wanted to tell you this was your best play.

JOHN: Easy to say, Dennis.

DENNIS: They recommended it to the Shuberts.

JOHN: The Shuberts?

DENNIS: They want the Shuberts to enhance their production. They told me to messenger them a script.

JOHN: Did you?

DENNIS: I did not.

JOHN: You didn't.

DENNIS: I *took* it over. Friday. Personally. And presented myself to the Shubert organization.

JOHN: What did they say?

DENNIS: They said, "Who the fuck are you?"

JOHN: Sounds like the Shuberts.

DENNIS: No seriously. They said somebody would read it that night.

JOHN: Easy to say, too.

DENNIS: Their head reader called me Saturday morning. John!

JOHN: And said?

DENNIS: She flipped!

JOHN: Seattle flipped on Thursday, the Shuberts flipped on Saturday.

DENNIS: She said a Shubert theatre might be available in early April. In time for the Tonys. Depending on how we do in Seattle, of course.

JOHN: Of course.

DENNIS: I tried to call your agent. But he'd gone for the weekend.

JOHN: You still never called me.

DENNIS: I kept *trying,* John. But this time your phone was out of order.

JOHN: Oh right. One of the grandchildren keeps playing with the portable.

DENNIS: We're talking Seattle and Broadway, John!

JOHN: I've never had a play on Broadway.

DENNIS: That I know.

JOHN: I know this sounds like sour grapes, but I've never really wanted it. All that noisy scenery rolling around. Those disagreeable ushers. And those peculiar audiences, Dennis. Who are those people? Who would I be talking to? They look like those types you see settling into first class when you're edging your way to the back of the plane. Everyone seems to be there on some special deal.

DENNIS: Most of them are, John.

JOHN: Broadway is bullshit, Dennis. *(Pause.)* Except I'd give my left nut to try it, once, before I die.

DENNIS: Here's your chance.

JOHN: Yeah yeah.

DENNIS: No, now listen. What would you say if I said…Robert Redford!

JOHN: Robert who?

DENNIS: Cut it out, John. The Shuberts want to send a script to Redford.

JOHN: Why?

DENNIS: Because he's looking for a play.

JOHN: Oh sure.

DENNIS: They *called* him, John! Out at *Sundance!* And told him about yours!

JOHN: I hear he refers to himself as Robert the Red. Like some Viking over-lord.

DENNIS: May I go on, please?…He told the Shuberts he was interested.

JOHN: You mean he didn't flip?

DENNIS: He hasn't *read* it yet. But he wants to. Immediately.

JOHN: Which, in Hollywood-speak, means maybe next year, after three more movies and two more divorces.

DENNIS: No, John, *no!* Because his *agent* called. Sunday *morning,* for God's sake! And reconfirmed. He said Redford was intrigued by everything he had heard.

JOHN: Intrigued is easy.

DENNIS: He might even do the tryout in Seattle if he likes the script.

JOHN: Big if.

DENNIS: There are always ifs in this business, John.

JOHN: *(Dryly.)* Oh really.

DENNIS: There's an if about me, for example. What if Redford doesn't approve of me.

JOHN: I approve of you.

DENNIS: You're not Robert Redford.

JOHN: Strange. My wife tells me the same thing.

DENNIS: But what if he vetoes me? I've never worked on Broadway.

JOHN: You've got a fine track record, Dennis.

DENNIS: In the provinces.

JOHN: You made a couple of my plays work that never worked before.

DENNIS: Redford doesn't know that.

JOHN: *I* know that. I'm committed to you, Dennis. Enough said.

DENNIS: That's what I told Redford's agent.

JOHN: And what did he say?

DENNIS: He said Bob would have to meet me.

JOHN: And what did you say?

DENNIS: I said I'd have to meet Bob.

JOHN: There you go!

DENNIS: And I said you'd have to meet Bob, too.

JOHN: I'll pencil Bob in.

DENNIS: You're so cynical about all this, John.

JOHN: I've heard it all before.

DENNIS: This one feels real.

JOHN: Did you get a script to Redford?

DENNIS: No.

JOHN: No?

DENNIS: Not yet.

JOHN: Why not?

DENNIS: Your ending.

JOHN: My ending?

DENNIS: Your ending's not right yet, John.

JOHN: Says who?

DENNIS: Says me. Says Seattle. Says the Shubert Organization.

JOHN: I thought they flipped.

DENNIS: Not about the ending.

JOHN: What's wrong with the ending?

DENNIS: Let's see. How do I put this?...It turns in, rather than out, John.

JOHN: You mean like a belly button?

DENNIS: It's too cozy, then. Too domestic. O.K., too sentimental, John.

JOHN: What's wrong with a little sentiment?

DENNIS: It's not you, John.

JOHN: It's me now.

DENNIS: O.K., then. It doesn't *work,* man! Your play is going in an entirely different direction. There you are, bopping along, heading bravely into new territory, and then suddenly—screeech!—you slam on the brakes, do this one-hundred-and-eighty-degree turn, and end up right where you started. Back in the bosom of the fucking family.

JOHN: What's wrong with the—family?

DENNIS: It's not enough, John. I've been there, believe me.

JOHN: I wrote that ending after I got out of the hospital.

DENNIS: I know that.

JOHN: It's the way I felt. The way I still feel, goddamnit. I've been recalled to life.

DENNIS: Oh Jesus. What's *that* from? "Recalled to life."

JOHN: Dickens again. *A Tale of Two Cities.*

DENNIS: Dickens was sentimental.

JOHN: Then I'm in good company. Oh look, Dennis, in the hospital, I felt pretty close to the edge. All I could think about was what I was leaving: Ellen, the kids, the whole shebang. And now I've got my reprieve—or what I hope is my reprieve—I want to go home.

DENNIS: It doesn't fit, John.

JOHN: With what?

DENNIS: With where you were going before.

JOHN: I think it does.

DENNIS: Why didn't you show it to your wife?

JOHN: Ah.

DENNIS: Yes. Ah.

JOHN: Because she might not like it, Dennis. She might find it a little…personal.

DENNIS: She won't like it because it's wrong, John! You cannot be a father and a writer at the same time! Shakespeare left his family in Stratford. O'Neill disinherited his kids. Your buddy Dickens turned his back on his wife and eleven children. You can't have it both ways. Art and life don't mix. You'll fuck up your play, you'll fuck up your family, you'll fuck up yourself.

JOHN: Who are you? The oracle of Delphi?

DENNIS: I am, in this. Now come on, John. Give us a final scene where you plug in a larger world. That's all we need. You could do it in your sleep, man!

(John makes a snoring sound.)

DENNIS: God! This is hard labor.

JOHN: Take a holiday. It's Labor Day.

DENNIS: Please, John. Seattle needs to set their fall schedule. And the Shuberts are known for their limited attention span. And me—I've got an interview in town at seven.

JOHN: Tonight? For what?

DENNIS: I have to keep my options open, John. In case this doesn't work out.

JOHN: Oh. Right.

DENNIS: So tick-tock, man. While I'm still young.

JOHN: I work slowly and carefully.

DENNIS: This, from the guy who wrote what could be a terrific play in less than six months!

JOHN: That was ages ago.

DENNIS: That was just last spring.

JOHN: That was when I was sick. And didn't know it.

(A knocking at the door.)

JOHN: I'm well now. *(Calls off.)* Come in.

(The door opens. Ralph comes in. He's in his mid-thirties, sweaty from tennis, still carrying his racquet. Swimming pool noises are heard from farther off.)

RALPH: Sorry to interrupt, Dad.

JOHN: Glad you did…Dennis, this is my older son, Ralph…named after Ralph Roister Doister, the first comic hero in English drama.

RALPH: Cut it out, Dad.

JOHN: Ralph, this is Dennis, my obstetrician.

RALPH: *(Shaking hands.)* Hiya, Dennis.

JOHN: What can I do for you, Ralph?

RALPH: Susie wants you to see her dive.

JOHN: Susie's diving?

RALPH: She thinks she's diving.

JOHN: That's good enough for me. *(Starting out.)*

DENNIS: Hey. I thought we were in labor here.

JOHN: Just a quick look. This is a major accomplishment for Susie.

DENNIS: John—

JOHN: Ralph, entertain Dennis while I'm gone. *(John goes, shouting.)* I'm coming, Susie, I'm coming!

(Pause.)

RALPH: Sorry about that.

DENNIS: Oh well.

RALPH: Susie's my daughter.

DENNIS: Ah.

RALPH: She likes to show off for Dad.

DENNIS: Oh?

RALPH: When she learned her ABCs, she sang them to him over the telephone.

DENNIS: *(Dryly.)* Sounds adorable.

(Pool sounds.)

RALPH: *(Glancing out the window.)* Want a beer or something?

DENNIS: No thanks.

RALPH: I've got a stash of microbrews back at the house.

DENNIS: No thanks.

RALPH: I can't get you a Coke. It's against my mother's religion. She goes ballistic over junk food.

DENNIS: Thanks. I've got coffee.

RALPH: So. You're directing a play of Dad's?

DENNIS: Trying to.

RALPH: This a new one?

DENNIS: Hot off the griddle.

RALPH: Is it good?

DENNIS: Best thing he's ever done.

RALPH: No kidding.

DENNIS: It just needs a little work, that's all.

RALPH: Dad's a good rewrite man.

DENNIS: That's what they say.

RALPH: He's like a good relief pitcher. Send him in, he saves the game.

DENNIS: So I hear.

RALPH: Once he wrote this terrible play, and the critics peed all over it, so he rewrote the whole thing top to bottom. Everyone said it was much better, though between you and me, it still sort of sucked.

DENNIS: That's good to know, Ralph.

(The sound of a belly flop from Susie, followed by groans from the adults.)

RALPH: What's it about, this new one?

DENNIS: He hasn't told you either?

RALPH: He never talks about his plays.

DENNIS: *I'll* talk about it, then. It's about us. Or could be.

RALPH: Us?

DENNIS: You, me, all of us, living in the United States of America, at the tail end of the twentieth century.

RALPH: Wow.

DENNIS: That's the way I see it, anyway. If I can just get him to nail it down at the end.

RALPH: He'll do it. You wait. He'll come through.

DENNIS: Let's hope.

(Another try by Susie; another splash; more groans from adults.)

RALPH: *(Wincing.)* Splat. Ouch…Any action in this play?

DENNIS: Action?

RALPH: You know. Action. Action.

DENNIS: Oh man, this has plenty of action.

RALPH: Cool! Normally Dad's plays don't have much action.

DENNIS: All your dad's plays have action, Ralph.

RALPH: No offense, Dennis, but I don't think so.

DENNIS: You're probably confusing action with activity. Lots of people make that mistake.

RALPH: Oh yeah? *(He tosses a dart or two.)*

DENNIS: Oh sure. For example... *(Indicating the dart throwing.)* That was what we call an activity.

RALPH: Yeah?

DENNIS: In the theatre.

RALPH: Yeah?

DENNIS: But it was not an action.

RALPH: I never said it was.

DENNIS: So what do you mean by action, then, Ralph?

RALPH: You know. Where things move. Where you have danger and suspense and that stuff.

DENNIS: Ah. See? You're thinking of action movies.

RALPH: Yeah?

DENNIS: Actually, those movies are more about activity than action, Ralph.

RALPH: I don't agree with you there, Dennis.

DENNIS: O.K. Name a movie you like.

RALPH: *The Terminator.*

DENNIS: *The Terminator.*

RALPH: *The Terminator* had really good action. So did *Terminator Two.* And *The Predator.* All had excellent action.

DENNIS: No, Ralph. Those movies are simply demonstrating *activity.* Demolishing cars. Breaking glass. Punching people up. But all that activity is not really action.

RALPH: I think it is.

DENNIS: Well it isn't. Action is basically different. Hold it, let me think... *(Thinks.)* O.K. Here's a simple example. You and I are playing this scene right now. Right?

RALPH: Scene?

DENNIS: Yes, consider this a scene between you and me.

RALPH: O.K.

DENNIS: Now your action in this scene—this is your action, Ralph—is to entertain me while your father watches your daughter dive into a pool. That's your action. O.K.?

RALPH: O.K.

DENNIS: Now *my* action—because I have an action here, too—my action is to persuade you that your dad is writing a good play.

RALPH: O.K.

DENNIS: So there are *two* actions going on here, Ralph. This scene has a double action, which makes it twice as good as most action movies, O.K.?

RALPH: O.K.

DENNIS: You're just saying O.K. because your action is to be accommodating. I don't think you really believe me.

RALPH: I don't, Dennis.

DENNIS: *(Thinking.)* O.K., then, I'll tell you something else, Ralph. Here's something that makes this scene even more complex. Here you have two characters, both male, both roughly the same age, confronting each other in the same room. One is tan from being outdoors, and basically interested in light entertainment.

RALPH: That's me, huh?

DENNIS: That's you. And the other is pale from being indoors, and basically interested in serious drama.

RALPH: And that's you.

DENNIS: Stop me if you think I'm railroading you.

RALPH: No, I'm with you, Dennis.

DENNIS: O.K. now. These two guys are having this scene. One is straight, married and the proud father of at least one child.

RALPH: Two, actually.

DENNIS: Two? Ah-hah. Well, the other guy is gay, scared of living alone, and involved in a relationship fast going sour.

RALPH: You gay?

DENNIS: I am.

RALPH: I didn't know you were gay, Dennis.

DENNIS: Well I am, Ralph.

RALPH: You don't seem gay to me.

DENNIS: You mean because I'm not pinning you spread-eagled across that desk?

RALPH: No seriously. I didn't pick up on that at all. *(He unconsciously moves farther away.)*

DENNIS: Thank you, Ralph.

RALPH: Gay, huh?

DENNIS: May I go on, Ralph?

RALPH: Sure…Gay…Hmmm.

DENNIS: May I continue, Ralph?

RALPH: Sorry. Go ahead.

DENNIS: So one of these guys is straight, and one is gay. One is the natural
    son of the writer involved, the other is the *artistic* son of the same man.

RALPH: Hey! I didn't think of that. That's interesting now.

DENNIS: And so these two actions I've been talking about, these conflicting
    actions, also contain an undercurrent of filial rivalry. You and I are locked
    in an ancient and deadly combat for the attention and approval of the
    father. To you, he's the father you must supplant... *(Noticing Ralph's ten-
    nis racquet.)* Just as you supplanted him this morning at tennis. To me,
    he's the father I never really had, whom I need to reach in some basic
    way. All of which makes this scene, if we play it right, Ralph, pulse with
    dramatic action.
    (Pause.)

RALPH: They talk a lot in plays, don't they?

DENNIS: Language is a major element in drama, yes.

RALPH: O.K. Now may I do some talking, Dennis?

DENNIS: All right.

RALPH: O.K. now. I go to all Dad's plays. O.K., he pays for the tickets, but I
    always go. And I get my friends to go, too. And I make them pay full
    price. And to be honest with you, Dennis, when we go out afterwards
    and talk things over, we all think Dad's plays are just a little bit slow.

DENNIS: I'm sorry you feel that way, Ralph.

RALPH: Yeah, but you're the director. You could do something about that,
    Dennis.

DENNIS: Such as?

RALPH: O.K. Let me give you an example. Are you a baseball fan?

DENNIS: Not really. No.

RALPH: That's cool. But maybe you'd agree that Dad's not fundamentally a heavy
    hitter.

DENNIS: Oh well...

RALPH: He's not, Dennis. *(Indicating posters on the wall.)* He hits singles or dou-
    bles primarily. He's sort of like Wade Boggs.

DENNIS: Who?

RALPH: Boggs. Wade Boggs. Played third base for the Red Sox, 1982 to 1990,
    then played for the Yanks.

DENNIS: Oh.

RALPH: Now Wade Boggs is good, Dennis. Not great, but good. He normally
    comes through in the end. Has some personal problems, but hell, who
    doesn't.

DENNIS: I'll go along with that.

RALPH: *(Taking up a pad and pencil; writing things down.)* O.K. So the life-time batting average of Wade Boggs comes to about, oh say, three twenty-five, three thirty, something in that area. Had an exceptional year in 1987. Won a Gold Glove in 1993.

DENNIS: Gold Glove.

RALPH: For third base. Never made M.V.P. Should of, in my opinion, but didn't. *(Writing on pad.)* O.K. Now over the years I've averaged out Dad's hits, runs, and errors, and if you take a look, you'll see he's somewhat in the same ballpark as Wade Boggs. *(Displays what he's written to Dennis.)* *(Pause.)*

DENNIS: They talk a lot in sports, don't they?

RALPH: About statistics, yes.

DENNIS: So what are you saying, Ralph?

RALPH: I'm saying, bring up Dad's average, Dennis. By putting in more *action,* Dennis! O.K., it's the wrong word, but whatever it is, put it *in,* man! Because that's what Dad needs. I'm serious. Otherwise he'll end up just another Wade Boggs.

(John's voice is heard offstage.)

JOHN'S VOICE: Hiya, Eddie.

RALPH: *(To Dennis; proudly.)* That's my son Eddie.

DENNIS: I can't do anything if he won't settle down and work.

JOHN'S VOICE: O.K., Eddie, one quick game of catch…

(We might see John behind, catching and tossing the ball.)

DENNIS: Ralph, I'll make a deal with you.

RALPH: A deal with me?

DENNIS: You're the oldest of the four kids, right? You're the leader of the pack.

RALPH: Well, my sister Ginny thinks she is. But I'm beginning to assume more responsibility.

DENNIS: I haven't met Ginny.

RALPH: We call her Little Hitler.

DENNIS: Little Hitler?

RALPH: Because she keeps suggesting we do things. And we always do them.

DENNIS: What a terrible name to call anyone.

RALPH: I know. She keeps suggesting we stop. So we probably will.

JOHN'S VOICE: *(From off.)* Good catch, Eddie!

RALPH: *(Looking out.)* Eddie's gearing up for Little League next year…

DENNIS: So here's the deal, Ralph. I'm not terribly interested in baseball, and you're not terribly interested in theatre. But we both want to see your dad get a hit. Right?

RALPH: Absolutely.

DENNIS: A home run, if possible.

RALPH: Of course.

DENNIS: O.K. Now he could easily hit a homer with this script.

RALPH: No kidding.

DENNIS: Easily. He could easily win...what is that gold thing?

RALPH: You mean, M.V.P. Most Valuable Player.

DENNIS: He could easily win the Broadway equivalent of M.V.P., Ralph, if we can come up with the right ending.

RALPH: All right then. Go for it.

JOHN'S VOICE: *(From off.)* Good throw, Eddie!

DENNIS: I can't, if we keep being interrupted.

RALPH: He *likes* being interrupted. Ever since he got out of the hospital, he keeps saying he can't see enough of us.

DENNIS: I know that, Ralph. But you could do him, and me, a big favor by keeping people away for the next hour or so.

RALPH: So you can work.

DENNIS: So we can make the *play* work. Now could you do that for me, Ralph? Even if somebody has just learned how to dive, or throw a baseball, or read the Cat in the Fucking Hat.

RALPH: Easy, Dennis. There are kids in the vicinity.

DENNIS: I'm just asking you to help me turn your father into who? Babe Ruth, rather than—what's his name?

RALPH: Wade Boggs.

DENNIS: Wade Boggs. Will you do it?

RALPH: If you'll put in more action.

DENNIS: I will, Ralph. I'll try.

RALPH: Then it's a deal.

DENNIS: Thanks, Ralph. And then opening night on Broadway, when the audience is cheering, and the critics are dashing up the aisle to write uniformly rave reviews, you and I will celebrate the occasion with a microbrew.

RALPH: I'd go to a gay bar, but I've got nothing to wear, Dennis.

DENNIS: We'll go to a sports bar, dude. And I'm paying.

RALPH: *(Giving him a vigorous high five.)* You're on, man!

(Dennis winces as John comes in.)

JOHN: *(Wiping his brow.)* Children are never more serious than when they're playing games...You're wanted at the pool, Ralph. Ginny wants a changing of the guard.

RALPH: *(He looks at Dennis.)* Right. I'll take over. *(He goes off calling.)* O.K., Ginny! The Varsity will take over!

JOHN: *(Looking after him; to Dennis.)* He's a good boy.

DENNIS: I agree.

JOHN: He's had his ups and downs, of course. Well, they all have. But he's in the groove now.

DENNIS: Seems to be.

JOHN: He's a civil engineer. Works for some company in Danbury. Wife works, too. Relentless life. Both up at the crack of dawn. She runs five miles, while he feeds the kids. Then *he* runs five miles, while she gets them on the school bus. Both arrive at work by a quarter to eight. Kids, some-how, get to day care in the afternoon. Parents take turns picking them up. Dinner together—very important. Chicken pot pies from the microwave, probably, but together. Then everyone does homework. Parents as well as kids. All in bed by nine, nine-thirty at the latest.

DENNIS: Stop!

JOHN: Weekends? Grocery shopping. Soccer or hockey for the boy. Ralph coaches. Swimming or gymnastics for the girl. Alice helps. Sometimes, Saturday nights, after the kids are in bed, Ralph rents a video.

DENNIS: *The Terminator.*

JOHN: Exactly. After a life like that, wouldn't you want to see things blow up? Of course, she prefers *The English Patient,* where things blow up more beautifully.

DENNIS: We should get to work.

JOHN: And yet. And *yet.* Through all that activity...

DENNIS: Good use of the word, John.

JOHN: Or rather in *spite* of all that activity, he still finds time to telephone us every Saturday morning. Eight-thirty A.M. Always calls. Always announces himself. "This is your son Ralph." Always says, "What's happening, Dad?" Always. When I was in the hospital, same thing. "What's happening, Dad?" *(Wipes his eyes.)* I'm sorry. I get a little teary these days. It's those female hormones they've been shooting into my ass.
(Pause.)

DENNIS: I haven't got all day, John.

JOHN: Right. Sorry. Let's go.

DENNIS: *(Getting out his notes.)* I'd like to walk you through some thoughts I have here. Just to jump-start you.

JOHN: Shoot.

DENNIS: *(Referring occasionally to his notes.)* All right. Here you have a guy...

JOHN: *(Laughing.)* Robert Redford.

DENNIS: *(Seriously.)* We hope Robert Redford…playing the governor of a large and populous state. And your story builds toward his keynote address at the Democratic National Convention.

JOHN: I know what I wrote, Dennis.

DENNIS: You do and you don't, John. You might not realize, for example, that you fall into three different modes of writing in this script.

JOHN: "Modes" of writing?

DENNIS: Attitudes, tones, whatever. You start off with the kind of stuff you can do in your sleep. We get a series of sardonic, slightly cynical scenes about contemporary manners and morals…

JOHN: I wrote that part before I knew I was sick.

DENNIS: O.K. But it works. So you're moving along smartly in this mode, and then we find out the hero is in mortal danger.

JOHN: That's when I got my bad news.

DENNIS: Good news for the play, John. You shift gears and everything changes. Your writing becomes rich and warm and expansive. And our hero's character expands, too. In all his scenes, he displays a wonderful kind of compassion for the human condition.

JOHN: I wrote that while I was being treated. I met all these nice people in the hospital, and in a support group afterwards…

DENNIS: There's where you really hooked me, John. And hooked Seattle and the Shuberts. And there's where you'll hook Redford. I mean, who wouldn't want to play a guy who bursts into bloom this way? It makes his keynote address thrilling!

JOHN: Thanks.

DENNIS: But then the play takes a final turn.

JOHN: When he goes home.

DENNIS: There's our argument, John.

JOHN: That's the part I like best.

DENNIS: That's the part I hate most.

JOHN: Give it a chance.

DENNIS: Oh sure. And get killed by the critics.

(Knocking.)

JOHN: Come in.

(Ellen comes in.)

JOHN: *(To Dennis.)* I can think of worse ways to die.

ELLEN: Telephone for you, Dennis.

DENNIS: *(Looking at John.)* It's Jason. I gave him your number.

ELLEN: Take it in our bedroom. It's relatively private.

DENNIS: Thanks. *(He goes.)*

ELLEN: If the dog's on the bed, kick her off!

JOHN: *(Calling after him.)* Ease her off, Dennis. Gently. *(To Ellen.)* She's a sweet old thing.

ELLEN: I don't want to talk about dogs, John.

JOHN: What better thing to talk about?

ELLEN: How come you didn't show me your play?

JOHN: Because it's not finished.

ELLEN: It's finished enough to give to Dennis.

JOHN: He's my director, darling.

ELLEN: I'm your wife, darling. And a little hurt.

JOHN: Oh come on.

ELLEN: You've never bypassed me before. I always get first crack.

JOHN: This one's different, sweetheart.

ELLEN: How? Am I in it?

JOHN: You are. In a way.

ELLEN: In what way? What do I do? Make coffee? Announce meals?

JOHN: You are the mainstay, darling. As you always have been.

ELLEN: Do you get into any of the bad times?

JOHN: What bad times?

ELLEN: We've had plenty of bad times, John.

JOHN: Well who hasn't? Thirty-five years and still counting.

ELLEN: You've never written about the bad patches.

JOHN: Thank God.

ELLEN: I wouldn't mind if you did.

JOHN: *I'd* mind.

ELLEN: Seriously, I sort of wish you would.

JOHN: Why?

ELLEN: Maybe I'd feel less conventional and middle-class.

JOHN: We are not middle-class, Ellen.

ELLEN: Oh no?

JOHN: We are *upper*-middle-class, and don't you ever forget it.

ELLEN: Whatever we are, I wouldn't mind if you showed us doing a little yelling and screaming.

JOHN: I don't intend to, thanks.

ELLEN: You know what I wish you'd show? That time I threw that soup bowl at you. Filled with celery soup.

JOHN: Impossible to stage, darling.

DENNIS: You never know till you try.

JOHN: Oh I could fake it, I guess, but we'd end up spouting a string of clichés, or staring at each other in total silence. Soap opera or Samuel Beckett, take your pick.

DENNIS: *(Thinking.)* O.K., then bring on the bad guy. End with the barbarian invading your circle of civility.

ELLEN: Earl is not a barbarian, please.

DENNIS: O.K. then make him—what? An emissary from the developing world! Give him a speech about human rights that will hurl us into the twenty-first century!

JOHN: I'm not that big a man, Dennis.

DENNIS: You're bigger than Wade Boggs, John.

ELLEN: What's wrong with Wade Boggs? I like Wade Boggs.

DENNIS: O.K., then something else…I'm just brainstorming here, but hey! How about that Lithuanian baby-sitter? Suppose you made her a secret terrorist from the former Soviet Union! Have Redford discover—

ELLEN: Dennis.

DENNIS: What.

ELLEN: Stop.

DENNIS: But this is my last chance to—

ELLEN: I know. But stop.

DENNIS: But if we can just nail down the—

ELLEN: I know. But still. Stop.

> *(Pause.)*

DENNIS: I'm pushing, aren't I?

ELLEN: I'm afraid you are.

DENNIS: I'm forcing things where they don't want to go.

JOHN: That might be the problem.

DENNIS: I got caught in the commercial thing. Result: chicken shit.

JOHN: The revenge of the chicken-house.

ELLEN: That's enough of that.

DENNIS: But it's true.

JOHN: That's the theatre, Dennis. Sometimes it's chicken shit, sometimes it's bullshit. Once in a while, it's more than that.

DENNIS: Yeah, well this I know: I'm not the man to direct your plays, John.

JOHN: Come on.

DENNIS: What's good to you is bad to me. And vise versa. We've both learned that today.

JOHN: You've made my stuff work, Dennis.

DENNIS: Yeah, by finessing the cozy element.

JOHN: No, no…

DENNIS: Hey, look. I'm a theatre man. I know when to bow out. *(Gathers up his things.)* I'll tell the Shuberts and Seattle we had artistic differences.

JOHN: You might add that I'm now totally hung up.

DENNIS: Thanks to me, right?

JOHN: You pried open some doors, Dennis. Now I can't close them.

DENNIS: Sorry about that. *(Starts out.)*

JOHN: It might do me good…How are you going to live?

DENNIS: I've got that meeting tonight, actually. With some folks from Houston. They want me to direct a one-woman show by a refugee from Cambodia.

JOHN: Is it good?

DENNIS: It could be. It's about how it feels to become an American.

JOHN: Sounds like something I should see.

DENNIS: Maybe you will. I think I've found a way to make it work. *(Starts gathering up his things.)*

JOHN: Dennis. Would you work with me again? If I get it all together.

DENNIS: I might. If you keep some of it apart.

JOHN: You'll be the first to know—I mean, after my wife.

ELLEN: Thank you.

DENNIS: *(Shaking hands with Ellen.)* Thanks for the great peanut-butter sandwiches.

ELLEN: Wonderful to have you here, Dennis.

DENNIS: *(Picking up script.)* Yeah, but was it?

JOHN: I'd walk you to your car, but…

DENNIS: That's cool. I'm going solo these days, remember? *(He goes.)*

ELLEN: What's this solo stuff? I thought he had a boyfriend.

JOHN: They're breaking up. Maybe we could fix him up with Scooter.

ELLEN: There's an ending for you!

JOHN: *(Indicating the wine.)* Want a little fortification before he shows up?

ELLEN: It might help.

(Ginny comes in, followed by Ralph.)

GINNY: We're getting ready to go.

JOHN: You too?

GINNY: The boys are exhausted. And Jeff flies to Cleveland tomorrow.

(Ginny and Ralph start tidying things up.)

RALPH: I've got a large-scale cleanup project in Bridgeport.

JOHN: Cleanup?

RALPH: That's what I do, Dad. Remember? Environmental work?

JOHN: Good Lord. I forgot.

ELLEN: Couldn't you all stay for a quick supper?

GINNY: It's better if the gang's not here when Scooter shows up.

ELLEN: Right as usual, Ginny.

RALPH: Scooter and I could handle the guy, Dad!

ELLEN: Stay out of it, darling.

GINNY: Mom, I froze the meatloaf and left that small chicken casserole in the oven for you and Dad. And the sheets are in the dryer.

ELLEN: I thought the dryer was broken.

GINNY: I fixed it. It was just a loose wire.

ELLEN: You are a godsend, darling.

RALPH: Dad, I checked your smoke alarms. They all needed new batteries. So I put them in.

JOHN: Thanks, man.

GINNY: I fed Mandy's kids. They're now watching *Bambi* with the au pair. I started the tape late, so they won't see where the mother gets shot.
    (Ralph and Ginny close the windows.)

ELLEN: Ginny, you think of everything.

RALPH: I turned off the outside water, Dad. Just in case. So your pipes don't freeze.

JOHN: I would have forgotten.

RALPH: I'll round up the kids. We'll honk when we're ready. *(Starts out, stops.)* Oh, and good luck tomorrow, Dad. I'll give you a call.

JOHN: Thanks, buddy.
    (Ralph goes.)

GINNY: Yes. Good luck, Dad. We're rooting for you. *(Starts out.)* See you at the car.

JOHN: Ginny...
    (She stops.)

JOHN: I haven't asked you much about yourself this weekend.

GINNY: My*self*?

JOHN: How are you, sweetheart?

GINNY: I'm fine, Dad.

JOHN: But I mean, are you happy?

GINNY: I am, Dad.

JOHN: Happy with Jeff? Happy with your children? Happy with your life?

GINNY: I am, Dad. Really. Thank you.

JOHN: Is there anything about you I should know, and don't?

GINNY: Yes.

JOHN: Tell me.

GINNY: Well. I've just decided this, actually. In a year or two, when the boys are settled in school, I think I'll run for office.

JOHN: Political office?

GINNY: The state legislature. Or maybe even Congress.

JOHN: I'm amazed.

GINNY: So am I. I figure if I have to play the go-between, I might as well do it big.

ELLEN: And get paid for it in the process.

GINNY: That, too.

JOHN: You'll win, sweetheart.

GINNY: Maybe. But now I've got to concentrate on car seats. *(She goes; we hear her calling.)* O.K., boys! Into the car!

JOHN: *(To Ellen.)* Did you know that about her.

ELLEN: I knew some West Side action group had approached her.

JOHN: I didn't know that at all. *(Pause.)* Good God, everything's happening under my nose, and I don't even know it. Ralph is cleaning up the environment, Mandy is exploring human rights, and Ginny is responding to political upheavals on the Upper West Side.

ELLEN: Don't forget Teddy.

JOHN: Teddy is still a saint.

ELLEN: Teddy's in jail, John.

JOHN: What?

ELLEN: Diane called. He was stopped for speeding on the Massachusetts Turnpike, and put up an argument.

JOHN: Good Lord.

ELLEN: The police asked her what his problem was. She said he was simply running away from his father. They understand that in Massachusetts. They'll fine him and let him go.

JOHN: See? I don't know anything. I'm not even sure I know you.

ELLEN: You know me well enough.

JOHN: Dennis was right. What made me think I could write about my family? Or anything else, for that matter. Me and my fucking circles of civility! I retreat to them every time. I've blown it. *(Indicating picture of his father.)* I can hear my dear, dead father whispering in my ear: "All right, John. Sit down. You've had your turn. Give someone else a chance." I hear you, Pop. I'll never write another play.

ELLEN: Yeah, yeah.

FRED: Either way, you're history, kid.

MONA: Fred—

HARTLEY: I can handle him, Mona.

MONA: All right, then I'll go shopping. Even though I feel extremely nervous about what might happen in the next scene. *(She goes.)*
(Hartley and Fred eye each other.)

FRED: *(Indicating the danger seat.)* Sit down, kid.

HARTLEY: *(Sitting.)* All right.

FRED: Tell me about yourself.

HARTLEY: I already did, at the restaurant.

FRED: Tell me more.

HARTLEY: O.K. I was born…

FRED: Cut to the chase, kid. How much do you contribute annually to the gross national product?

HARTLEY: Well I hope someday to—

FRED: Do you consume?

HARTLEY: Do I…?

FRED: Buy things? Use things? Throw things away?

HARTLEY: Well I…

FRED: You're in graduate school, aren't you?

HARTLEY: I was. I…

FRED: Old man pay the bills?

HARTLEY: No, as a matter of fact, I got a…

FRED: Government loan?

HARTLEY: No, a personal…

FRED: Ever thought of paying it off?

HARTLEY: Of course I'll…

FRED: Do you work?

HARTLEY: I do some undergraduate…

FRED: Call that teaching?

HARTLEY: I like to think…

FRED: How many hours a week do you so-called teach?

HARTLEY: Nine or ten, counting…

FRED: I work nine or ten hours a *day!*

HARTLEY: You don't have a thesis to…

FRED: My father worked eight days a *week!*

HARTLEY: Well, we live in different…

FRED: My grandfather worked fifty-two weeks a year, and never took a vacation, except once, to Ocean City, New Jersey, when he rode the Bump-Mobiles.

HARTLEY: We're getting off the subject, Fred. I have a proposal to make.

FRED: You want to change something? *(To audience.)* The graduate school grunt, who has never met a payroll in his life, wants to change the world.

HARTLEY: Oh come on.

FRED: *(To audience.)* Young Lochinvar out of the east wants to reinvent the wheel.

HARTLEY: Oh now please…

FRED: My wife Bernice and I were among the first subscribers to this theatre. We sit in the same seats every year.

HARTLEY: Congratulations.

FRED: When we need subscribers, Bernice gets on the phone. When we run a deficit, Bernice gets out the checkbook. When we need a benefit, Bernice makes the macaroni salad.

HARTLEY: Yes well I happen to think…

FRED: Do you realize that since our guest lecture series, the crime rate in this town has decreased thirty-nine percent?

HARTLEY: I don't think…

FRED: We have fourteen percent fewer divorces! Seventy-three percent of our youngsters now go to college, and sixty-two percent of these can read!

HARTLEY: I don't see…

FRED: Eighty-*six* percent of our senior citizens are continent! Forty-one per-cent of the time! Poverty has gone bye-bye. Homelessness is a no-no. Welfare is pee-pee, poo-poo, ca-ca. And listen to this, sonny boy: Our two-bit minor league ball club has made the interstate finals four out of the last six years. In 1997, we scored three consecutive runs on a full-court press, without even icing the puck!

HARTLEY: I didn't know that.

FRED: There's a lot you don't know, sonny. Why do you think these things happen? Because this community has had the guts to get together once a year in this theatre, and do a little spring cleaning.

HARTLEY: Ah. You're talking about catharsis.

FRED: Come again?

HARTLEY: Catharsis. Aristotle called it catharsis.

FRED: *(To audience.)* Mr. Peepers comes up with a new word.

HARTLEY: Not a new word, sir. A very old word. Aristotle argued that good theatre had a *cathartic,* or purging, effect on the *polis,* or city, cleansing it of its aggressive or selfish instincts and recementing its communal bonds.

FRED: Give it whatever cockamamie name you want, son, the thing works.

HARTLEY: May I have the floor now, please?

JULIA: I suppose you expected him to place it on a silver tray in the front hall.

ANDERSON: That's the tradition, as a matter of fact. He should have presented himself.

JULIA: This isn't Annapolis, Jim. And we're not still fighting the War of 1812.

ANDERSON: The nerve of the guy!

JULIA: I'll bet you would have done the same thing yourself. In your flyboy days.

ANDERSON: Send a sailor? Hell no! I would have sent a Marine. *(Sits on the daybed.)*

JULIA: He wrote a very sweet note on the back. *(Reading.)* "I apologize for my absence on the 4th. I have no excuse but my own negligence."

ANDERSON: He didn't neglect some B-girl on the beach.

JULIA: Don't tell me he's already found one.

ANDERSON: So he says.

JULIA: What is it about these women?

ANDERSON: Don't ask me.

JULIA: Why not ask you? I believe you're familiar with that particular scene.

ANDERSON: Long ago and far away.

JULIA: At least he took her seriously.

ANDERSON: Seriously?

JULIA: An Academy man would have broken the date. For the sake of his career.

ANDERSON: Julia, honey, these Newport types take nothing seriously. They hop on board for a little R and R, and then jump ship to go home and make their pile.

JULIA: He already has a pile, if I've got the right family. They own a whole beer company in Milwaukee.

ANDERSON: I don't give a shit what he owns, as long as he does his job. Now let's not worry about the kid. *(He downs his drink, takes his glass offstage.)*

JULIA: I'm afraid we have to. For just a tad longer.

ANDERSON: *(From off.)* Why?

JULIA: I sent him a note, asking him for a drink.

ANDERSON: *(Returning.)* When?

JULIA: Tonight.

ANDERSON: For Chrissake, Julia!

JULIA: I had to do *something*, Jim. He left a calling card.

ANDERSON: *(Indicating the card.)* Look at the corner! It means no answer is required.

JULIA: Well you see I didn't know that, Jim. I'm not privy to all these dumb

Navy rules. Besides, I know his family. It won't kill you to have a short drink with one of your junior officers.

ANDERSON: Except I won't be here.

JULIA: Hey! We have a date tonight.

ANDERSON: Date? Date?

JULIA: The movies at the Officers' Club.

ANDERSON: Oh God.

JULIA: Remember?

ANDERSON: They've called a joint staff meeting up in Tokyo.

JULIA: On what?

ANDERSON: Indochina.

JULIA: Don't tell me we're going in *there*.

ANDERSON: *(Checking contents of briefcase.)* We're making contingency plans.

JULIA: We're not even out of Korea.

ANDERSON: This looks like more of the same shit. Admiral Radford wants to bomb, you know.

JULIA: Bomb who?

ANDERSON: I'm not even sure.

JULIA: What a bunch of blowhards we are!

ANDERSON: I'll convey your opinion to our Task Group.

JULIA: Will you be back tonight?

ANDERSON: First thing tomorrow.

JULIA: Are you sure you don't have some B-girl on the beach?

ANDERSON: Trust me.

JULIA: I shouldn't, but I do. So go to Tokyo. While I struggle through an awkward half hour with— *(Looks at card.)* What does he call himself?

ANDERSON: Sparky. Sparky Watts.

JULIA: I'm sure it's the same one.

ANDERSON: *(A quick kiss.)* Have fun. *(He goes.)*
(Clack. Julia stands looking at the calling card.)

READER: Officer here, Okusama.

JULIA: Send him in, Noriko.
(Clack. Drumming, lights change. Sparky comes on, looking resplendently innocent in his dress whites.)

SPARKY: *(Saluting.)* Mrs. Anderson, I presume.

JULIA: Welcome…Now. Would you mind if I gave you some quick advice, right off the bat?

SPARKY: Shoot.

JULIA: *(Taking his hat.)* Never salute a woman. Never wear your hat indoors. And never wear dress whites on unofficial occasions.

SPARKY: Oh, I know all that stuff. I just thought the captain might get a kick if I went whole hog.

JULIA: *(Putting his hat on a stool.)* The captain couldn't be here.

SPARKY: Uh oh. Is he trying to avoid me?

JULIA: Either that, or he's trying to avoid a Communist takeover in Southeast Asia.

SPARKY: I'm not sure he likes me, anyway.

JULIA: He doesn't think you're serious about the Navy.

SPARKY: I am, though. I consider this to be one of the most formative periods in my life.

JULIA: Did you tell him that?

SPARKY: I did.

JULIA: Don't any more.

SPARKY: I hear you.

JULIA: What would you like to drink?

SPARKY: Whatever you're having.

JULIA: A gin and tonic. It's the latest thing.

(A Stagehand enters with two gin and tonics on a tray.)

JULIA: The British drank it in Singapore to ward off malaria.

SPARKY: How does it do that?

JULIA: The quinine in the tonic. But maybe it's just an excuse to get sauced.

(She hands him a glass, takes one herself.)

SPARKY: Who needs an excuse?

JULIA: There you go.

(They toast each other.)

JULIA: But now we have to play a short, brisk game of Do-You-Know.

SPARKY: Shoot.

JULIA: I hear you're celebrated throughout the free world as "Sparky" Watts.

SPARKY: I am.

JULIA: And you're also from Milwaukee.

SPARKY: Correct.

JULIA: Do you know a family there named Brandt? Of Brandt Beer?

SPARKY: My mother was a Brandt.

JULIA: I roomed with Emily Brandt at Westover School. And again at Smith.

SPARKY: Emily Brandt is my mother's younger sister!

JULIA: We were good friends. I visited her in Milwaukee before the war. I went to all the dances. She showed me your family compound on Lake Michigan. It was quite a spread, I might add.

SPARKY: I'm trying to get away from all that.

JULIA: All that's a lot to get away from.

SPARKY: Yeah well out here I'm beyond the pull of gravity.

JULIA: Emily wrote you were coming to Japan.

SPARKY: I'll bet my mother asked her to.

JULIA: I'll write back that I've tracked you down.

SPARKY: Say hi for me, O.K.

JULIA: I'll say I'm keeping an eye on you.

SPARKY: Keeping an eye on me?

JULIA: She asked me to.

SPARKY: Oh hell. That's just Milwaukee talk, Mrs. Anderson. Just say I'm doing fine.

JULIA: I'd rather say I'm bringing you into the fold.

SPARKY: What fold?

JULIA: This fold. Right here. On the base.

SPARKY: Uh-oh.

JULIA: It's sort of my job, actually, as wife of a senior officer. I'm supposed to encourage younger officers to enter in. Do you play bridge?

SPARKY: I'm a passable bridge player.

JULIA: Which means you're good.

SPARKY: Which means I pass.

JULIA: Oh now stop. What else do we have?...A sailing group. I got the Navy to ship over six Penguin-class dingies, and we have sailing races every Sunday in Tokyo Bay.

SPARKY: No thanks.

JULIA: Oh come on. I imagine you tooted all over Lake Michigan in some Brandt boat.

SPARKY: I get bored on a sailboat, Mrs. Anderson.

JULIA: What? A Navy man? Then there's the book club, but I'll bet you're out of our league, being fresh from Princeton. And there's always a tennis tournament of some sort.

SPARKY: I've already entered the singles.

JULIA: Good for you! And we have Sunday softball games. I've worked it so women can play, and it's lots of fun. And there's even a Bible-reading group which frankly I do NOT recommend.

SPARKY: Halleluia.

JULIA: How about another drink? You can't fly on one wing, as Jim keeps saying.

(A Stagehand brings two more gin and tonics.)

SPARKY: *(Furtively checking his watch.)* Maybe a quick one.

JULIA: *(Taking a glass.)* Where did you find her, by the way?

SPARKY: Who?

JULIA: Madame Butterfly.

SPARKY: Oh. We kind of found each other, actually.

JULIA: At the Kit Kat Club?

SPARKY: No.

JULIA: I'm surprised. That's the usual meeting place, isn't it? I hear there's a woman there named Frenchy, who's had her eyes rounded and her breasts built up. Isn't she the one who usually comes up with the girls?

SPARKY: I wouldn't know.

JULIA: Where else, then? The Blue Note? The Cherry Blossom? The Ichi-Ban Numba One Hot Bath and Massage Club?

SPARKY: I didn't meet her at any of those places, Mrs. Anderson.

JULIA: Don't be scared of shocking me. I know what goes on.

SPARKY: You sure do.

JULIA: I'm not like those Navy wives who trot endlessly back and forth between the Officers' Club and the PX, never glancing beyond the gate. In fact, I'm not really a Navy wife at all.

SPARKY: Oh?

JULIA: I'm what's known as a Second Wife. I strive to be different.

SPARKY: I can see that.

JULIA: Before I was married, I had a career of my own. I worked for the Voice of America.

SPARKY: Hey. Great.

(They sit side by side on the "couch.")

JULIA: Oh sure. Two years ago you would have found me in the Philippines, setting up a new radio station. I met Jim when he came steaming into Manila Bay on the *Intrepid*. He was an Air Group Commander and very dashing.

SPARKY: I'll bet he was a wild man.

JULIA: He was not.

SPARKY: Don't kid me. I've seen these carrier pilots hit the beach.

JULIA: He had just lost his only son over North Korea.

SPARKY: Oh. Sorry.

JULIA: Shot down by the Chinese.

SPARKY: Oh boy.

JULIA: Jim was devastated. He had been divorced for years, but now he needed…well, I guess he needed to hear the Voice of America. And there I was, itching for a change. They had just promoted this political hack over my head, and I was fed to the teeth with the flitty State Department bureaucracy. I suppose I could have stayed and fought things out, but…

SPARKY: Shazam! Captain Anderson to the rescue!

JULIA: Well, one thing led to another rather quickly. As can happen in the Far East. As you well know.

SPARKY: I do.

JULIA: So the Navy gave him shore duty, and here we are. *(Pause.)* But he can't get over Korea.

SPARKY: Now I know why.

JULIA: You should also know that he's a very nice man. He just wants to be in the air again, or at least at sea. He doesn't like being anchored to a desk.

SPARKY: *(Getting up.)* I better go.

JULIA: *(Getting his hat.)* Hey, have you seen *From Here to Eternity?*

SPARKY: Damn right. Sinatra's fantastic.

JULIA: Want to see it again? We could have a quick bite first at the Club. I'll introduce you around.

SPARKY: I can't, Mrs. Anderson.

JULIA: You're tied up?

SPARKY: I'm tied up.

JULIA: With your newfound friend?

SPARKY: Right.

JULIA: Is she the most attractive thing in the world?

SPARKY: I think so.

JULIA: How can I compete with that?

SPARKY: You don't have to, Mrs. Anderson.

JULIA: Your family would want me to. What do I write Emily?

SPARKY: Don't write her anything.

JULIA: I promised I would.

SPARKY: Say I've entered a tennis tournament.

JULIA: I'd like to say I've taken you in tow. *(Thinks.)* What if I say you've joined our new dance class?

SPARKY: Dance class?

JULIA: I'm getting the U.S.O. in Tokyo to send us a dance instructor once a week, to teach us all the new steps from the States.

SPARKY: I'm not much of a dancer, Mrs. Anderson.

JULIA: One night a week? We need men desperately.

SPARKY: Who would I dance with?

JULIA: There are plenty of pretty girls on this base, Sparky. There's a nurse named Cricket, who's absolutely divine.

SPARKY: I hear she's taken.

JULIA: She *is*. By that stupid Bible class.

SPARKY: There you are.

JULIA: Because you young officers won't give her the time of day.

SPARKY: I'm taken, too, Mrs. Anderson.

JULIA: I won't tell Emily that, if you come to dance class.

SPARKY: Is that a promise.

JULIA: Cross my heart.

SPARKY: One night a week.

JULIA: That's all.

SPARKY: It's a deal.

(*They shake hands.*)

JULIA: I'll write Emily that I found you playing tennis and going to dancing school.

SPARKY: They'll go for that in Milwaukee. (*Starts out.*)

JULIA: And you won't get stuck, I promise.

SPARKY: Thanks for the drink, Mrs. Anderson.

JULIA: I can't believe that you haven't seen one woman on this base who is even remotely attractive?

SPARKY: Sure I have.

JULIA: And who, pray tell, would that be?

SPARKY: You, Mrs. Anderson.

JULIA: I see you learned to be polite in Milwaukee.

SPARKY: Good night, Mrs. Anderson. (*Sparky goes.*)

(*Clack.*)

READER: Julia? It's Esther! Are you decent?

JULIA: Always. That's my problem.

READER: I just wondered if you're playing bridge tonight.

JULIA: Not tonight, Esther. Tonight I'm seeing *From Here to Eternity.*

READER: By yourself?

JULIA: I'm getting used to that.

READER: It's terribly sexy, Julia. She goes swimming at night with an enlisted man.

JULIA: Sounds like just my meat. (*She goes.*)

(*Clack. Music. Stagehands convert the day bed into a barracks bunk as Bob,*

GRANDMOTHER: That's enough, Ed, please. You're making Annie uncomfortable.

EDDIE: *(To audience.)* Annie didn't like wisecracks about the Pope.

GRANDFATHER: And this is the wishbone which I'll put aside to dry. What's the dessert today, Madeleine?

GRANDMOTHER: Mrs. Driscoll has made a lovely Floating Island.

GRANDFATHER: Ah hah. Floating Island! Then after we've had that, Eddie, select two of your guests to make a wish on the wishbone.

GRANDMOTHER: Nancy, you're responsible for passing the gravy, and Eddie, send around that currant jelly. And I want you all to know Mrs. Driscoll made these rolls fresh this very morning.

GRANDFATHER: If anyone bites into a piece of shot, don't worry. It won't kill you.

EDDIE: It killed that duck, though.

GRANDMOTHER: It most certainly did, Eddie. A beautiful mallard duck, with bright green feathers.

GRANDFATHER: Just harvesting nature's crop, Madeleine.

GRANDMOTHER: Oh is that what you're doing? I never was quite sure.

EDDIE: Tell us about your hunting trip to Africa, Gramp. *(To audience.)* My grandfather shot lions in Africa, and big-horn sheep in Alaska.

GRANDMOTHER: I've had enough of guns and killing, please. I want to know about school. Is Miss Tilly still there?

EDDIE: Oh boy. She sure is.

GRANDMOTHER: Miss Tilly taught me, you know.

GRANDFATHER: Taught me, too, as a matter of fact.

GRANDMOTHER: Is she still trying to get rid of our Buffalo accents? *(She recites with a British accent.)* Who killed Cock Robin? I, said the sparrow, with my bow and arrow. I killed Cock Robin.

EDDIE: *(Equally affected.)* And there weh, in the same countri, shepheds, abiding in the fields...

EDDIE AND GRANDMOTHER: ...keeping wawch over their flawks by night.

GRANDFATHER: A toast to Miss Tilly!

EDDIE, GRANDFATHER, GRANDMOTHER: *(Together.)* To Miss Tilly!

EDDIE: *(To audience.)* And back at school everyone would come up to Nancy and me and beg to have lunch with my grandparents. We were very popular.

HARVEY: *(Calling out.)* I'm home! Where is everybody? Jane? Tim? Anybody?

EDDIE: *(Calling out.)* I'm in the living room, in case anyone's interested! Doing my geography! *(Memorizing.)* Maine, Augusta, on the Kennebec…New Hampshire, Concord, on the Merrimac…

HARVEY: Where's your lovely mother?

EDDIE: Taking a bath…Vermont, Montpelier, on the Winooski…

HARVEY: Run upstairs and tell her I am about to make her the finest cocktail in the Western World.

EDDIE: I have to memorize my states, capitols, and streams.

HARVEY: Eddie! When your father asks you to do something, you don't argue, you don't procrastinate. You simply leap to your feet and do it!

EDDIE: O.K., O.K., I'm going.

JANE: Never mind. Here I am.

HARVEY: How lovely you look, darling.

JANE: Thank you.

HARVEY: You might be interested to know that I've just had a drink with Roger Woodrich.

JANE: You didn't.

EDDIE: Uncle Roger?

HARVEY: I believe I was talking to your mother.

JANE: Don't interrupt, Eddie. If you plan to use the bookcase, fine. But be quiet, please.

HARVEY: He called me at work and asked to meet for a drink.

JANE: Not at the Saturn Club, I hope. Father's there every evening.

HARVEY: We met downtown at the Statler Bar. And had a perfectly nice talk. He wanted to clarify his intentions.

EDDIE: What does that mean?

HARVEY: Eddie, go upstairs and get some work done.

EDDIE: I am working…Rhode Island, Providence, on Narragansett Bay…

JANE: People always work better in their own rooms, Eddie.

EDDIE: *(To audience.)* So I went. Slowly.

HARVEY: He's decided to marry her.

JANE: Decided? How big of him!

HARVEY: Frankly, I thought it might just be a fling.

JANE: He's certainly had plenty of those.

HARVEY: He says they'll get married as soon as they've worked out a prenuptial agreement.

JANE: Knowing Mother, she'll hand him the moon.

EDDIE: *(To audience.)* On the landing, I accidentally dropped my book.

HARVEY: Eddie! I thought I told you to go upstairs!

EDDIE: That's where I'm going!

HARVEY: Then go, please. Right now.

EDDIE: *(To audience.)* Gram and Uncle Roger got married in Mexico. Nobody was invited, and Gram said she didn't even wear a veil.

JANE: *(To Harvey.)* Sooner or later I'll have to tell Father.

HARVEY: Chad Warren told him last night at the Saturn Club. Took him into the billiard room and spelled the whole thing out.

JANE: How did he take it?

HARVEY: Someone had to drive him home.

JANE: Oh no.

EDDIE: Why didn't he drive himself home?

HARVEY: Where did you come from?

EDDIE: I'm hungry.

JANE: Go tell Mabel we're ready, Eddie.

HARVEY: That boy is an eavesdropper. Every time we sit down for a cocktail there he is.

JANE: He's interested in Father. He adores him.

HARVEY: Why?

JANE: Why? WHY?

HARVEY: I mean he's a perfectly nice man, but…

JANE: He's a marvelous man! You see his name on plaques all over the city! Tennis, golf, squash, skeet-shooting! He can do anything he sets his mind to.

HARVEY: Except ride horseback.

JANE: He could do that, too. He just doesn't want to.

HARVEY: All right, darling. All right.

GRANDMOTHER: Eddie! Guess what, dearie. I have bought a horse! A big, gentle, lovely hunter with an easy gait and a smooth canter. Do you like to ride, Eddie? Do you, Tim?

EDDIE: Tim's scared to ride.

GRANDMOTHER: I used to be. But now it's my favorite thing.

EDDIE: Why?

GRANDMOTHER: Because you're free when you ride. You can go anywhere you want.

EDDIE: Can you jump over fences?

GRANDMOTHER: I'm learning. Your Uncle Roger takes every jump, and I'm trying to follow him.

EDDIE: Aren't you scared you'll fall off?

GRANDMOTHER: Petrified. But that makes it thrilling. It opens up a whole new world. It's certainly better than having to huddle shivering in some duck blind.

EDDIE: I think girls like riding more than boys, Gram.

GRANDMOTHER: Then tell you what. We'll let your sister Nancy do the riding, and you boys can do something else. Because Uncle Roger and I are making some big changes out here. We're redoing the house, and putting in a tennis court and a swimming pool and a special lawn just for croquet.

EDDIE: Will you put in a trout stream?

GRANDMOTHER: No, dearie. I don't believe we'll do that.

EDDIE: Gramp's taking me trout fishing some time.

GRANDMOTHER: You'll have plenty to do out here, Eddie, without hooking some poor fish.

EDDIE: What if I put some trout in the swimming pool?

GRANDMOTHER: No fish in my pool, please, I never want to see another fish in my life.

EDDIE: You could fish for trout any time you wanted.

GRANDMOTHER: Are you teasing me, Eddie? You are, aren't you?

EDDIE: Sort of.

GRANDMOTHER: Well don't, dearie. Please. These days I've got enough on my mind without people teasing.

EDDIE: *(To audience.)* I wish this could be a movie so they could show this camp my grandfather has on Big Rock Lake in the Adirondacks. He inherited it from Old S.S. It's very wild up there. There's no electricity, which means kerosene lamps, and getting your water from the lake, and having to use an outhouse. There are lots of trout in the lake, and deer come down to drink, and once when my mother was a little girl up there, she saw a bear. *(To Harvey and Jane.)* Can I ask Gramp to take me to Big Rock this summer?

HARVEY: I wouldn't.

JANE: It might do Father some good. He hasn't been there since Mother left.

HARVEY: The plumbing is nonexistent, Eddie. And it rains incessantly.

JANE: Why don't you want him to go, Harvey?

HARVEY: Because he'd be bored out of his mind, if he's anything like me.

EDDIE: I'm not like you.

HARVEY: I'm beginning to discover that.

JANE: I'll speak to Father.

GRANDFATHER: Big Rock with Eddie? I'd like that.

EDDIE: Yippee!

JANE: Here's a chance for you to light a fire under him, Eddie.

HARVEY: But don't bring up your grandmother.

EDDIE: I won't, Pop. I'm not that dumb.

HARVEY: Sometimes I wonder.

EDDIE: *(To audience.)* Gramp and I took Route 20 east. And the farther we got from Buffalo, the more Gramp talked.

GRANDFATHER: See that? That is the old Erie Canal. That canal was built so that goods coming from Europe could come up the Hudson, swing past Albany on to Buffalo, and then onto the Great Lakes and out West. And products from the West came back through Buffalo, on down the Hudson, and all over the world. Old E.G. was working on a farm when he saw them building that canal. Knew a good thing when he saw it. Put down his plough, moved to Buffalo, married a rich girl, started a bank, got the city to dredge a harbor, helped finance it. Ran for Mayor. Ran for State legislature. Ran for Congress. Won every time. Served in Lincoln's cabinet. Taught Lincoln a thing or two about money.

EDDIE: Did old E.G. get rich?

GRANDFATHER: Rich as Croesus. The city wanted him to donate a library, but he refused. He said he had already donated his time and services, and saw no further reason to diminish his pile.

EDDIE: *(To audience.)* We stopped by a lock, and watched a boat go through.

GRANDFATHER: Just the occasional pleasure boat these days.

EDDIE: *(To audience.)* We drove north, past Utica, along West Canada Creek up into the mountains. *(To Grandfather.)* Why are we stopping at this little cemetery?

GRANDFATHER: See those two gravestones? Off in the corner? Those are for Elmer and Buck. They were our guides. Hired by my father.

EDDIE: Old S.S.?

GRANDFATHER: Old S.S. hired Elmer and Buck. They were a special breed, those Adirondack guides. They built our camp, made our boats, made our furniture, taught me about the woods. Once my father said, "What do you plan to do with your life? Do you want to go into business? Do you want to learn a profession?" And I said I just wanted to stay at Big Rock and work in the woods with Elmer and Buck.

EDDIE: *(To audience.)* We sat for a while, just looking at those gravestones. *(To Grandfather.)* Are you all right, Gramp?

GRANDFATHER: I'm fine. *(Blows his nose.)* On to Big Rock…Once, when Elmer and I were digging the foundation for the boathouse, I found two Indian arrowheads. Which made me realize that long before Old S.S., long before Elmer and Buck, the Indians were up here, catching Big Rock trout.

EDDIE: *(To audience.)* We parked at the landing. The caretaker left a boat so we could row over to our camp. After he cooked supper, Gramp showed me how to work the kerosene lamps.

GRANDFATHER: Do you want a light by your bed?

EDDIE: I do, Gramp. It's sort of scary upstairs.

GRANDFATHER: Take it, then. I'll blow it out when I come up.

EDDIE: Don't you want a light down here?

GRANDFATHER: No. I'll just sit and look at the lake.

EDDIE: *(To audience.)* And I heard him making a drink in the dark…And in the morning…

GRANDFATHER: All right, Eddie, up and at 'em.

EDDIE: What are you doing to those hooks, Gramp?

GRANDFATHER: Clipping off the barbs, so it's a fair fight…Now hop in the canoe. I'll do the paddling, you do the casting…Gently…don't be a water-slapper…Lay it quietly over by that lily pod…Now raise the tip of your rod. Slowly, slowly…There! See? A strike!…Good! You've hooked him… Keep the line taut now…Ease him alongside the boat so I can net him… That's it, that's it!

EDDIE: *(To audience.)* And he taught me how to clean them and cook them for breakfast…

GRANDFATHER: Leave the heads and tails on.

EDDIE: Why?

GRANDFATHER: So we'll remember that what we're eating was once beautiful and alive…And don't put so much butter in the pan. Big Rock trout have a taste like nothing else in the world, and you don't want to ruin it…

EDDIE: *(To audience.)* Twice at night we went out jacking deer…

GRANDFATHER: Sit here in the stern, between my knees…Ssshhh…quiet…

EDDIE: *(Whispering.)* Gramp used a jacking paddle which he carved out of ash-wood when he was just my age…

GRANDFATHER: *(Whispering.)* Hear that? That's a deer drinking…Now I'll shine my light and there! See?…A three-point buck!

EDDIE: Could you shoot him?

GRANDFATHER: At night? With a light? Wouldn't be sporty…Now look at the sky. Let's learn our constellations…

EDDIE: *(To audience.)* And we went camping overnight, and Gramp showed me how to do a front flip off a rock, and one night, we just read books by the fire.

GRANDFATHER: Look at this old Atlas, Eddie. Read what it says about Buffalo.

EDDIE: *(Reading.)* "Queen City of the Great Lakes…located at the mouth of the Niagara River…Named after a Seneca Chief named Buffalo, or possibly for the bison herds who originally roamed the area." *(To Grandfather.)* I thought Buffalo came from the French. Beau Fleuve, beautiful river.

GRANDFATHER: Where'd you get that?

EDDIE: Gram said it, actually.

GRANDFATHER: Some people like to gussy things up. Read on.

EDDIE: *(Reading.)* "…A teeming, muscular metropolis, with a rough past and a ready future. Sixth largest city in the United States." *(To Grandfather.)* Our teacher said we're only thirteenth.

GRANDFATHER: That's because we're being passed by.

EDDIE: Why?

GRANDFATHER: Some say the railroads took over from the canal, and went on to Chicago. Some say our weather is inhospitable. Whatever the reason, we've lost our usefulness.

EDDIE: Can we get it back?

GRANDFATHER: People are trying. But sometimes the world just passes you by. It's a law of life.

EDDIE: What's that noise, Gramp?

GRANDFATHER: That's just a beaver, smacking his tail.

EDDIE: You're sure it isn't a bear?

GRANDFATHER: Oh no. The bears are passing us by, too. Things are getting too fancy for them. I hear the Albrights are putting in a pump.

EDDIE: *(To audience.)* Our last day at Big Rock it rained…

GRANDFATHER: If you'll excuse me, Eddie, I'll row over to the landing and hear the news from Europe on the car radio.

EDDIE: *(To audience.)* So I found an old snapshot album and looked at pictures of the old days. And guess what? I found a picture of four people, out in the sun, on the front steps of our camp. There was my Grandmother, looking young and pretty, smiling and hugging her knees. Next to her was Gramp, with his arm around her. Standing behind, with his hand

1

A NEW AGE,
A NEW
CURRICULUM

Science has nearly always been taught in elementary schools. Children learn about plants, animals, rocks, and stars. They draw pictures and hear stories about objects in their environment. Simple experiments are performed, sometimes having to do with very complex ideas. For the most part children are interested in and enjoy science, but somehow, in these activities the spirit and meaning of science is frequently missing. What children do in class, the stories they read, the pictures they draw, the experiments they perform are more ends in themselves than means to understanding the natural world. If we assume children should understand a society that is largely oriented toward science—their world—it seems that science teaching will need to be different from that of the past.

The age of science, which journalists sometimes call the "atomic age," the "space age," the "age of automation," or the "computer age," represents a new phase of history. It is a period characterized by atomic energy, biotic drugs, and new elements. It is a time in which science is having considerable influence on human affairs—social, economic, and political. All of this suggests that children need to know considerable science to understand the culture of which they are a part.

The challenge of devising and testing a new curriculum in elementary science has attracted the interest of scientists and educators alike. The question is whether children can learn authentic science in the elementary grades and whether the content can be taught in an honest way, so that it will not have to be retaught in later years.

SCIENCE TEACHING FOR AN AGE OF SCIENCE

The children today live in a new world of science, and it is getting "newer" every day; there are new discoveries, new medicines, new ways of doing things, new kinds of jobs. One has the impression that we are living in a very dynamic time of history. And this is so; life today is radically different from that of the past. But the question in the minds of many parents, teachers, and scholars is whether the science curriculum is keeping pace with the world of their children. There is also the question of what the goals of science teaching should be for a rapidly changing society, for a civilization that produces new knowledge faster than it can be either communicated or consumed. Developing a new science, called information retrieval, has become necessary to help keep track of existing knowledge. Since a child is in class for only a relatively short period, what should we choose to teach from all the science that is known? How should it be taught and under what instructional conditions? However one looks at these questions, it becomes apparent that the traditional elementary school science curricula are seldom adequate in concept or purpose to help children meet the demands of our modern scientific-technological-industrial society. Without new approaches to elementary school science teaching, we run the danger of having children become strangers within their own culture.

The Knowledge Explosion

It is important to take a closer look at the "knowledge explosion" in science. We all vaguely know that there is more to every aspect of science than one could learn in a lifetime. How can an elementary school curriculum be designed that is up-to-date, when the amount of scientific knowledge doubles in the time it takes a child to progress from kindergarten to high school? What kind of instruction is needed for today's children, who before middle age will have access to eight times as much knowledge as there is currently? Is it possible to invent a science curriculum for use in the elementary school that will enable one to live comfortably and meaningfully with science and to appreciate its changing system of concepts, theories, and methods? This is an intriguing goal, and some of the curriculum research groups think it can be realized.

SCIENCE AND MANKIND

Over three centuries ago the British philosopher Sir Francis Bacon predicted that science would someday contribute greatly to the betterment of man's material world. With the advancing years of the twentieth century, science and its application in technology have helped to make this vision a reality. Together, science and technology have speeded communications and transportation, have made food more abundant and diseases easier to control. Work has become less exhausting, and we all look forward to a longer life. In thousands of other ways as well, science and technology have combined to make the world a better place in which to live.

Science and technology influence our lives in indirect ways. The ability of a country, through good school and college programs, to educate scientific and technical manpower and to achieve a high level of scientific literacy has much to do with the economic success of that nation. How successful we are depends to a great extent upon the public's appreciation of the value of scientific research. The development of atomic power, the exploration of space and the oceans, the use of satellites as communication centers and weather-observing stations are examples of science and technology supported at public expense. These developments form the base of much of what we mean by the modern world.

Over the past 500 years science has come to influence many areas of intellectual life. Western man aspires to be objective, to make decisions in terms of valid evidence, and to use the scientific approach in acquiring new information. The success of science as a means for understanding the natural environment has given people almost unquestioning faith in the potential of science in all areas of learning.

Since the middle of this century, it has become increasingly apparent that with the growth of modern science there must be new approaches to the teaching of science in elementary schools. In response to this need, scientists, educators, and psychologists have cooperated in formulating a number of new proposals for elementary science instruction. These innovative programs differ from usual offerings in that they have been developed to teach science in the way it is known to scientists. This innovation raises the question of what has been taught under the name of science in the elementary school.

WHAT SCIENCE IS

Focusing on the dictionary meaning of science rather than on its true nature, textbooks for children often treat science as a body of information. Thinking exclusively of science as a "body of knowledge" restricts its meaning. History, for example, is a body of knowledge but is not considered a science. One characteristic of science is its concern with natural events that can be observed repeatedly. The historian, on the other hand, must be content with investigating events that occur only once and cannot be reproduced. His ideas and hunches about the interrelationships of past events are not subject to experimental test. In science the situation is different. If a biologist wishes to determine the effect of Vitamin A on an animal, he can vary the amount of the vitamin in the diet of several groups of test animals. And if the animals are very much alike and are treated identically, he can observe the effects of increasing, decreasing, or entirely eliminating the vitamin. Interested scientists can repeat the experiment on other animals until considerable confidence can be placed in the knowledge obtained. In this way, through verifying experimental results, the knowledge about our natural world has grown.

Making Scientific Knowledge Useful

Scientific knowledge is more than a mere accumulation of bits and pieces of information; it has a conceptual organization. As observations and experimental data are gathered, sometimes over a period of many years, they become organized into concepts or principles that not only describe what is known but often suggest where to look for new information. Some examples of science concepts are the following:

Animals obtain energy by changing foods chemically.
Living things exhibit a diversity of type and a unity of pattern.
The total amount of matter and energy in the universe is unchanging.
Change is universal.
The position and motion of an observer influence his observations.

Concepts in science arise from an organization of data and observations that makes these discrete pieces of information more useful and meaningful. Consider the variety of observations that can be acquired from a visit to a zoo. We see many animals, each with differing features and colors. What meaning can be gained from these observations? Why, for example, are animals so diverse in their coloring? If we relate an animal's color to its natural habitat, we can begin to see the advantages of certain color patterns. It becomes clear why the ptarmigan changes color in winter and summer. It can blend into its native surroundings and, therefore, is less easily seen by predators. But what about the bold stripes of the tiger or the brilliant colors of the macaw? Since we now have some idea (concept) about animal coloration and its relation to the animal's natural environment, we suspect the stripes of the tiger and the color of the macaw have something to do with where these animals normally live. In other words, we have a notion about where to look for an answer to our question. In fact, we may be able to derive a fairly accurate answer. Depending upon our background of experiences, it may occur to us that the home of tigers is in brush and tall, thick grass, where vertical stripes tend to blend into the background; thus the tigers move about with less likelihood of being detected. The macaw's bright plumage protects him in a tropical environment by confusing potential enemies; the bird is not clearly visible when sitting among the brilliant blossoms of jungle trees. From many observations we thus arrive at the concept: *Colors help protect animals in their natural environment.* In this way knowledge in science is organized, and from that organization comes the power of science for explanation and interpretation. It is not facts that characterize science but the organization we give to facts.

Science as a Process

The most distinguishing characteristic of science is its methods. The gathering of facts or the making of observations is only the starting point of science. Science is an activity that takes place in the minds of men; it is the result of certain *intellectual processes* that make discovery possible. The processes of science are the means by which scientists examine the unknown, the procedures researchers use to investigate the natural world. For example, without the careful measurements of the physicist and the chemist and the close observations of the biologist, the natural environment would soon cease to yield useful information. Measurement and observation are among the basic processes that research workers find useful. It is difficult to teach people how to do science, but we can describe some of the abilities that are needed: (1) the ability to grasp the central theme of information about the natural environment, such as plants, animals, earth, the universe, the human body, and weather and climate. Health, safety, conservation, foods, care of pets, use of tools, and other applications of science were taught in connection with appropriate topics.

Emphasis on "doing experiments" characterized the elementary school science textbook and local courses of study for this period. A range of activities such as reading a thermometer or a compass, making a telegraph key, making a map of the planets, collapsing an oil can, "exploding" a volcano, using a magnet were available for almost every day of class. Then there were the birds, flowers, leaves, rocks, insects, airplanes, and other things to observe, comment about, and frequently draw. The "activity movement" in elementary education had found its way into the teaching of science, and the relationship seemed to be a very natural one—children learning through their own activities with materials of science. Frequently, these activities were associated with "problem-solving," as "What materials do magnets attract?" or "Can we show that air exerts pressure?" (the collapsing-can exercise). There is little question that these activities are fun, exciting, and cause discussion. But do they represent science? To those who know science best, the professional researchers, these activities have little relation to what scientists do. To those interested in the intellectual development of children, there is little in these activities that might contribute to this growth.

A curriculum reform in science teaching began at the secondary school level in 1957, and by 1960 there was a demand for an improvement in the teaching of science to grade school children. Some of the questions that were being asked of curriculum developers were these: (1) Can real science, science as it is known by scientists, be taught to children? (2) Are there certain prerequisites to the learning of science that children must first acquire? (3) Can we teach children science with curriculum materials that have a conceptual structure? (4) How can science be taught to advance the intellectual development of children? No one seemed to have answers to these questions; some teachers and scientists had ideas, and most were of the opinion that "something must be done."

The debate about the teaching of science in elementary schools became widespread. New science courses, reflecting a modern point of view, were successfully produced for use in the high schools. Teams of scientists and teachers working together wrote and tested new courses, and they have been widely adopted in schools. At the high school level, courses in earth science, biology, chemistry, and physics could be identified with corresponding disciplines, and the task of developing new courses was mostly one of preparing materials that represented the current methodological and conceptual structure of the discipline. But simply doing this was a major change from the way high school science courses had previously been organized. Nevertheless, it was evident that this approach could not be used for the elementary school, where the curriculum pattern is a selection of topics based upon criteria other than those characteristic of the discipline alone.

The concern about the teaching of science in the elementary school reached a point in 1960 when it seemed desirable to explore the issues in considerable detail. At this time the American Association for the Advancement of Science (AAAS) was asked to conduct a feasibility study to determine what needed to be done and how best to carry it out. Three conferences were held, the first in St. Louis, the second in Berkeley, California, and the third in Washington, D.C., to explore the issues. There were approximately 50 participants at each of these conferences, including a well-known scientist as the chairman, elementary school teachers and principals, specialists in science education, and scientists representing the major fields of science. Working papers were prepared for the conference participants that summarized the current status of objectives, course content, textbooks, facilities, instructional patterns, and organization of science in kindergarten through grade 6 and separately for grades 7, 8, and 9.

At each of these three-day conferences, four major issues were explored in depth: (1) What underlying philosophy and what aspects of science should be basic to elementary school science instruction? (2) What problems exist regarding instructional materials, such as textbooks, resource units, films, facilities, and equipment? (3) How should a national effort related to elementary school science curricula be organized and developed? (4) What improvements are desirable and practical in teacher preparation and programs for elementary school science teachers? Following the discussion on each of these questions, recommendations and suggestions for the improvement of science instruction in the grades were made. The participants agreed that science, including its concepts and methods of inquiry, could be taught to children in ways that are consistent with the meaning and spirit of modern science.

The 1961 regional conferences strongly recommended a large-scale, coordinated, and cooperative attack upon problems of elementary school science teaching. Several projects were already under way at various university centers, and it was felt that those projects should be encouraged to continue in their efforts to develop new course materials. It was clear from the feasibility conferences that alternate courses and blocks of instructional materials were more desirable for each grade than a single science curriculum. So that there might be some coordination of efforts, however, it was proposed that a national commission should be established to "work closely with the several centers both in initial planning and throughout the developmental program."

The *Commission on Science Instruction* was appointed by the AAAS in May 1962. The commission's activities were the following:

1. Maintain a continuous review of work being done under its own and other auspices and of the kinds of additional work that would most effectively supplement what has already been started.
2. Develop interest within the scientific community and recruit scientists to work on the development of elementary and junior high school science materials.
3. Arrange conferences, communication, and exchange of materials as the need arises among various groups working in this area.
4. Serve as an advisory body upon request to persons interested in the establishment of new programs or centers for the development of elementary or junior high school science materials and to agencies considering giving financial support to such ventures.
5. Provide interpretation and help to schools in the selection and use of new science materials.[24]

Other purposes of the commission included the development and production of teaching aids, evaluation, and curriculum materials as they might be needed to improve instruction in science.

One of the first activities of the commission was holding two eight-day summer conferences, one at Cornell University and the other at the University of Wisconsin, to explore in detail questions on the purposes, objectives, scope and sequence, laboratory experiences, and instructional units for elementary school science. The conferees included scientists, psychologists, elementary school teachers and administrators, and specialists in science and teacher education. At the

[24] *Science Education News* (Washington: American Association for the Advancement of Science, Dec. 1962), p. 2.

a particular operation or procedure of science to show how it may be applied in many different situations. For example, there are special units on observation, while others are exclusively on measurement. In a second type of unit, children learn to apply basic skills in limited contexts, such as measuring time or observing motion. Other units are on ways of using several operations in the study of a single science topic. Units on the study of symmetries and one relating to changing and unchanging properties are examples of this type. However, the distinction among the various kinds of units is not sharp, and in all units there is an attempt to provide a generous interplay between fostering science concepts and developing skill in using the processes or operations of science. Although the science and mathematics phases are not coordinated topic by topic, they are presented in a compatible spirit and in similar terms. This kind of presentation allows pupils to become aware of ways in which mathematics helps in science by providing techniques for managing data and to realize that science provides many opportunities to use mathematics.

Instructional Materials

Five types of instructional materials have been prepared to assist teachers using the MinneMAST science program. A *Teacher's Guide* for each of the units presents a general introduction to the topic and has specific suggestions for teaching the sequence of lessons that comprises the unit. For each lesson instructional materials are listed, and the procedure for using them is precisely stated. The Guide offers the teacher suggestions on how to arrange instruction, significant questions to ask children, and how to introduce the lesson. These materials are especially helpful to teachers with a minimal background in science or mathematics. By carefully specifying the techniques of instruction, the project writers hope to communicate the teaching approach required for a valid presentation of MinneMAST units. Once the purposes of a unit are clear and compatible instructional procedures identified, the suggested procedure can be looked upon as one example of what teachers might do in class.

Pupil work pages are available to provide pupils with practice in applying scientific skills and using the concepts they have learned. *Stories* relevant to the lessons have also been prepared. These may be used to illustrate applications of the topic under study. The Minne-MAST program provides materials to keep parents informed about teaching objectives and the new approaches to school work being used with their children. *Letters* have been written for the teacher to send home. These suggest ways parents can be of assistance in supporting the school's math-science program.

Recognizing that most elementary schools have not been designed to accommodate a "laboratory" type science program, MinneMAST has developed *special equipment* that can be adapted to any classroom situation. For example, reaction trays are available for chemical experiments. These trays are made of clear plastic, and each has several depressions, or small cups, in which chemicals can be placed and reactions observed. Since the reaction trays are inexpensive, they may be thrown away after the experiment, and thus most of the clean-up work is eliminated.

The following are among the elementary science materials that have been produced by MinneMAST:

Kindergarten
Watching and Wondering
Describing and Classifying
Our Senses
Shape and Symmetry

Grade 1
Objects and Their Properties
Changing and Unchanging
  Properties
Introduction to Measurement
Time: Measurement of Duration
Locating Objects
Investigating Systems

Grade 2
Measuring Weight
Scaling and Representation
Time-Ordered Events
Observing Motion

Grade 3
Related Properties
Discovering Systems
Time Rates and Time
  Dependence
Investigating Systems in
  Stationary States

Sample Lesson

The following sample of MinneMAST materials is from the first unit in the second-grade program. The unit begins with a review of some earlier activities, including observation and comparison of objects according to certain properties. Length is emphasized as a property that permits quantitative treatment and the ordering of objects as the basis of measurements. Weight is introduced as another example of measurement. A simple beam balance is used, by which objects can be compared and ordered according to weights. The children use the balance and a set of weights to design and carry out simple experiments.

LESSON 3: USING THE PROPERTY WEIGHT TO ORDER OBJECTS[39]

Teacher Commentary

In this lesson, the children are confronted with the problem of comparing two objects that are nearly alike in weight. They probably have already discovered in their take-home work that it is often difficult to distinguish which of two objects has the greater weight simply by holding them in their hands. The two objects they are asked to compare, a ping-pong ball and a paper cup, were selected because their difference in weight is hard to detect by "hefting." Discussion of this problem will develop the need for some weighing device that is more accurate and dependable than the hands. Encourage the children to suggest improved ways of comparing the weight of two objects other than by lifting. At this point, lead the discussion away from traditional scales with their standard units of pounds, ounces, etc., and direct the children instead to consider simple methods of *comparing the weight of two objects*. Part II of the "King Snooky" story presents this problem in an imaginative setting and leads to the suggestion of using a seesaw as an arrangement which can compare the weights of two objects rather well. The children take home copies of Part II, at this time, to add to Part I.

They are now challenged to use a ruler and other materials to make a balance with which to solve the problem of comparing the weights of the cup and the ball for themselves. The important relations for the equal arm balance are developed. With the understanding of these relationships, the children use the crude balance to order five objects by weight. The results of the comparisons are recorded by each child on Record Sheet #5.

In summary, the objectives of Lesson 3 are:

1. to develop the need for the beam balance to compare the weights of objects; and
2. to give the children experience with its use in ordering objects by weight.

An indication of the success of the lesson is the skill which the children demonstrate in using the simple seesaw for this purpose.

[39] From *Measuring Weight* (Minneapolis: Minnesota Mathematics and Science Teaching Project, 1966), pp. 22–25, S9–S12. Reprinted by permission of the University of Minnesota.

Procedure

Materials per group of four:

Plastic ruler
2 pencils, labeled *p* (new, hexagonal)
White chalk (new piece), labeled *w*
Scissors, labeled *s*
Ping-pong ball, labeled *b*
2 seven-ounce paper cups, labeled *c*
Part II of "King Snooky," Record Sheet #5 in workbook

If possible, provide a seesaw for the class or construct a simple one according to the plan shown here:

Sturdy plank about
6' x 8" x 2"

Brick (fulcrum)

Floor

Figure 4.23

Activity A. The completed take-home activity sheets from Lesson 2 provide a good starting point for this lesson. In discussing the sheets, lead to a review of the ideas of properties and the criteria used to order objects by such properties. Probably some of the children had difficulty deciding which of two objects has the greater weight. If this problem does not arise naturally in your group, do not press the matter. Rather, confront the children with two objects of nearly the same weight (the paper cup and the ping-pong ball) and challenge them to detect which object has the greater weight. (Always use the terms "greater weight" or "less weight" rather than "heavier" and "lighter." The former expressions tend to strengthen the connection between the inequality symbols and the words for which they stand.) When uncertainties or disagreements about the weights arise, ask for suggestions about how this difficulty could be cleared up. Commend thoughtful suggestions— especially use of a letter scale or a scale of any sort.

If someone suggests a seesaw arrangement, that is fine. In any case, read Part II of "King Snooky," pausing after paragraph 2 of page S-10 to give the children the opportunity to guess what playground equipment the prince and princess are using. If a seesaw is available, let the children use it to decide which of two children has the greater weight. Repeat this several times with other children. (Some of the important relations developed further along in the lesson may evolve at this point and you can stress these now, or not, as seems appropriate.)

Activity B.   Follow up the story, or seesaw activity, by giving each group of four children these materials: two new pencils, a plastic ruler, a ping-pong ball, and two paper cups (of roughly the same weight as the ball so that it is difficult to tell which has the greater weight). Challenge the groups to discover ways to decide whether the ball has greater or less weight than the cup. Possible solutions:

1. Ruler over pencil as seesaw.
   Two variations: Equal-arm balance—imbalance: object of greater weight down. (Best arrangement for our purpose.)
   Unequal-arm balance—balance: object of greater weight nearer the fulcrum.
2. Balance one object on ruler over pencil or edge of desk, etc.; then similarly balance the other object. Again the object of greater weight will be nearer the fulcrum.
3. The children may come up with other good ideas. Compliment them for any thoughtful suggestion.

Suggest that the equal-arm seesaw arrangement of the ruler over the pencil is a convenient method. Lead the discussion to emphasize the following ideas, having each tested as it is discussed:

a. Objects must be at equal distances from the fulcrum. (Show that this is true when two "identical" objects balance.)
b. An imbalance indicates unequal weights.
c. The lower end has the object of greater weight.
d. The raised end has the object of less weight.

Activity C.   Issue to each group the materials of Activity B, plus the white chalk and scissors. Have each group use equal-arm balance (ruler and pencil) to order five objects (ping-pong ball, pencil, chalk, paper cup, scissors) by weight. Have each child record the results of the comparisons on Record Sheet 5. Do the first one or two comparisons as a demonstration and show exactly how they should be recorded. Have the children do the remaining comparisons, recording their results.

TEACHER'S ANSWERS TO RECORD SHEET #5 FOR LESSON 3

NAME _____

COMPARING THE WEIGHT OF OBJECTS BY A SIMPLE BALANCE

W_w . . . . weight of white chalk

W_s . . . . weight of scissors

W_p . . . . weight of pencil

W_b . . . . weight of ping-pong ball

W_c . . . . weight of paper cup

$$W_b < W_c < W_p < W_w < W_s$$

or ($\geqslant$)

$$W_p > W_c$$
$$W_s > W_c$$
$$W_c < W_w$$
$$W_c > W_b$$

Children's Story: King Snooky and the Problem of Weight

A few days after King Snooky had visited Annabella-della at her shop, she sent word to him complaining about another problem. She asked if he would mind coming to see her again. If he could not come to help her, she said, she would not be able to pay her tax. When King Snooky received this message, he leaped on his horse and rode as fast as he could to Annabella-della's G.M.R.W.S.R.J. Shoppe.

Annabella-della quickly explained her problem to King Snooky. "Now that the new record system is so well known and admired, many of my customers want to be sure that they are getting the best object I have in the shoppe. I can sort the objects by size, by hardness, and by thing from a unit or go about it in the same way. In sequential programs such as SCIS and *Science—A Process Approach,* it is necessary for children to learn the material from the beginning because concepts and skills are built from simple forms into increasingly more complex structures. The SSCP program, on the other hand, is based upon the "discrete" unit idea. A scientific concept is incorporated into each teaching unit rather than using a continuum of units to build an idea. There is little agreement on the best means to account for individual differences, but the need to do so is implicit in each of the new curriculum studies.

A plan for individualizing instruction as a way of meeting differences among pupils is found in the *Oakleaf Individualized Elementary Science Project.*[2] Bringing together the framework and learning materials of *Science—A Process Approach* and the Science Curriculum Improvement Study, the designers of this program are developing and testing what is known as "science laboratory" lessons. With these each child, guided by tape-recorded directions, moves at his own rate through laboratory-based learning activities. The Oakleaf project is only one of several attempts at designing curriculum materials specifically to accommodate individual differences. Other examples include the Portland (Oregon) *Teachers Automated Guide* in elementary and junior high school science and the American Institutes of Research *Project PLAN* in science, mathematics, social studies, and language arts.

The experience to date seems to indicate that the new science curricula provide a way of meeting some of the differences in children's achievement, especially those dependent upon reading skills and verbal fluency. Thus, children with limited capabilities in these areas are often successful with the new science materials. The reason for this success is that the new curricula are based upon direct experiences; the observations are those of the children and are not solely dependent upon prior knowledge and language skills. The observations are then used to develop language skills. Talented children, on the other hand, can be challenged by the same materials, since it is possible to develop concepts and processes at a variety of levels of sophistication.

[2] Joseph I. Lipson, "An Individualized Science Laboratory," *Science and Children,* 4:8–12 (Dec. 1966).

SCIENCE AND OTHER SUBJECTS IN
THE ELEMENTARY SCHOOL CURRICULUM

Science for all children that is regularly scheduled in the curriculum is a distinguishing characteristic of the modern elementary school. Unfortunately, in too many instances this means a crowding of other subjects for instructional time. Over the past half-century the curriculum of the elementary school has grown by accretion; as social demands made it evident that children would need to acquire new experiences, they were added to the existing curriculum. Seldom does one finds that units or subjects were removed. What is more important, the traditional elementary school curriculum package and its organization have not been seriously examined in this century, although the need to do so is a problem that is debated continually in the educational literature. It appears that the 1970s will be a decade of curricular reform in the elementary school. There are already the "new" math, the "new" elementary science, the "new" social studies, a humanities program at various stages of experimental development available for preliminary planning in reshaping the elementary school curriculum.

Several approaches to the problem are presently available for exploration and consideration. One is bringing science and mathematics into a closer relation. Several of the new science projects use a quantitative approach to science teaching, and the MinneMAST materials for the early grades are definitely written to combine science and mathematics. The "new" science has already been shown to be highly effective in building children's vocabulary. Reading skills are of several kinds, and science materials provide one resource for developing some of these skills. With the subjects now in the elementary school, there are many opportunities for bridges between one subject and another. These are natural relationships in which the conceptual development of one topic is reinforced or expanded by experiences with materials of a different subject. For example, what significant social studies concepts can be derived from the observation that the history of modern science coincides in time with the history of America, or what understanding of the solar system is dependent upon having some concept of time and space relations?

It may be more desirable in reorganizing the elementary school curriculum to build it around intellectual skills and competencies rather than subject-matter topics. Three possible areas could be the cognitive, the affective, and the aesthetic. Since there are overlapping goals from science, social science, mathematics, and other fields, it is not unreasonable to expect that these goals, such as critical thinking or problem-solving, might form the basis of instruction. The AAAS *Science—A Process Approach* provides a model for organizing a curriculum around intellectual skills. Extensions to this program are possible; for example, *communication* as a "subject" is a goal of science, art, music, mathematics, social studies, and languages. Essentially then, this "subject" is a goal of the elementary school, one in which children learn to communicate in many ways, each depending upon what he wishes to communicate. It is quite possible that it is more effective and efficient to teach communication in a range of contexts that are mutually supportive than to focus the curriculum on diverse subjects in which communication is a goal.

A curriculum planned in terms of long-range goals from kindergarten through grade 12 could greatly increase, through improved sequencing and the elimination of mere repetition, the time available for each subject. Rather than repeating topics to help assure retention, important concepts would be revisited at several grade levels, each time in a new context for extending their meaning.

As progress is made in each of the new elementary school curriculum studies, it becomes increasingly evident that the total curriculum needs reconsideration. There is no reason to expect that the pattern for the first half of this century is adequate for the second half. The increase in new knowledge, the changing social and personal demands, the new concepts about learning and other educational forces provide impetus for a curricular reorganization in the elementary school.

IN-SERVICE EDUCATION

The new science represents a significant departure from previous programs. The content is novel, its organization is different, and the desired style of teaching varies from that generally practiced in elementary schools. Assuming that every teacher will be able to use the new approach without assistance in understanding the rationale, content, and essential teaching procedures is, therefore, unfair and unrealistic.

Where does the responsibility lie for in-service training programs?

Teacher-training institutions often hesitate to provide courses in how to teach a specific new curriculum. These institutions assume their role is more general: giving teachers a broad background that will enable them to use a variety of approaches. Schools, on the other hand, often lack the personnel needed to conduct extensive in-service training efforts. One way of providing in-service programs is for schools and colleges to plan together. A few model *cooperative training programs* of this kind have been developed in which a school district and a nearby college share personnel and resources.[3] Moreover, school districts can develop and use the leadership potential of their own staffs. Teachers, supervisors, or principals with an interest and background in science can be given time to learn more about the new curricular approaches and to help other teachers in using them. Using outside consultants or adding a science specialist to the school's staff is also a possibility. Unfortunately, the supply of curriculum specialists in science is very short, and the school will probably need to examine other means. Some of the new programs include preliminary plans for developing self-instructional, in-service materials for use by teachers. These materials consist of science experiences for teachers in terms of reading, laboratory experiments, and instructional films designed to acquaint the teacher with both the substance and the pedagogical aspects of the new curriculum. There are also films showing experienced classroom teachers working with children in a style compatible with the new program.

PRE-SERVICE TEACHER EDUCATION

Since the new elementary science requires different teacher competencies, pre-service teacher-education programs will need to be different. Two of the essential elements that need to be considered are the background science courses for elementary school teachers and the nature of the professional training. Teachers will need to have a background in science, to be sure, but this background should come in courses that emphasize the major concepts and principles of science. These courses need to be taught in a way that enables the teacher to experience and understand some of the intellectual struggle and the logical arguments that gave rise to these concepts and princi-

[3] H. J. Hausman, "The Cooperative College-School Science Program of the National Science Foundation," *Science and Children*, 4:26–27 (Mar. 1967).